Guide for Covenant Discipleship Groups

Gayle Turner Watson

DISCIPLESHIP RESOURCES

P.O. BOX 340003 • NASHVILLE, TN 37203-0003
www.discipleshipresources.org

This book is dedicated to members of my Covenant Discipleship Groups
in North Carolina, Texas, Tennessee, and Maryland,
who have watched over me in love,
holding me accountable for my own discipleship
as we journeyed together.

Reprinted 2001.

Cover and book design by Sharon Anderson

Edited by Debra D. Smith and Cindy S. Harris

ISBN 0-88177-305-0

Library of Congress Catalog Card No. 99-68754

DR305

Contents

Part 1

Why Covenant Discipleship Groups?

As the Father has loved me, so I have loved you; abide in my love. If you keep my commandments, you will abide in my love, just as I have kept my Father's commandments and abide in his love. . . . You are my friends if you do what I command you.
(John 15:9-10, 14)

Introduction

A Wesleyan Tradition

In 1975 the first Covenant Discipleship Group was formed in a local congregation: Holly Springs United Methodist Church in Holly Springs, North Carolina. Members who were a part of this first Covenant Discipleship Group had no intention of designing a program for the church. Their only desire was to have fellow Christians accompany them on their journey in discipleship, friends in the faith who would hold them accountable for their day-to-day efforts to follow the teachings of Jesus Christ. This modern adaptation of the early Methodist class meeting enabled people to experience the unique Wesleyan tradition of watching over one another in love, just as their Methodist forebears had done in eighteenth-century England and America.

Covenant Discipleship Groups have been formed in countless United Methodist congregations, on seminary and college campuses, and in a number of sister Methodist churches around the world. Knowing that Jesus Christ always needs reliable and dependable disciples, these groups use the method of Methodism, methodical discipleship, to meet the expressed need of Christians who want to make a deeper commitment to their faith. Such a commitment to discipleship needs all the help the church can give, but resources for discipleship training are seldom clearly defined.

In response to our consumeristic society, the church has developed a vast array of church programs intended to entice people to follow Jesus. But Jesus never used enticement. He never used pressure, logic, guilt, or any other kind of persuasive techniques to recruit disciples. When calling people to committed discipleship, Jesus used the direct approach. He used it two thousand years ago, and he uses the same direct approach today, saying simply, "Follow me." Those who are ready follow willingly. Those who are not ready are allowed to refuse. Jesus accepts our no as freely as he welcomes our yes. The one answer Jesus cannot accept is the one we offer when our biggest concern is keeping all options open. Jesus cannot accept "I'll think about it."

Covenant Discipleship Groups are designed for Christians who are ready to say yes in a new way, Christians who have reached a point in their faith journey where they wish to become more reliable and more dependable in their discipleship. Like early Methodists, Christians today know that the best way to live as reliable and dependable disciples is to have companions along the way. By joining with other Christians in a weekly meeting, members of Covenant Discipleship Groups learn to center their lives on Jesus Christ by following his teachings and supporting one another in living out the basics of Christian discipleship.

This handbook is primarily a practical reference manual for starting, developing, sustaining, and incorporating Covenant Discipleship Groups into the mission and ministry of the church. The first section of this handbook deals with the "why" of Covenant Discipleship and centers on the nature and purpose of being a Christian in the world of today. In the words of John Wesley, Christian discipleship is a matter of "heart and life." What we believe is important. What we do with our beliefs is equally important.

The second section answers the basic question, What are Covenant Discipleship Groups? It also addresses questions and objections that have been raised most frequently about groups in the past. Interestingly, these questions and objections are not new to our generation. They have been around as long as Methodism has been in existence. In fact, these same questions and objections have been around as long as the gospel itself. In addition to describing what Covenant Discipleship Groups are, this chapter also states clearly what they are not. Christians search for a sense of community in small group activities, so it is helpful to know what each type of group is—and is not—intended to accomplish.

The third section deals with the practical details of forming Covenant Discipleship Groups, writing a covenant, running weekly meetings, and perhaps most importantly, integrating them into the mission and ministry of the congregation as a whole.

The fourth section offers suggested resources for further reading, sample covenants, and other helpful information.

A key point in this book is that Covenant Discipleship Groups are intended to focus on entire congregations and not simply on groups of individuals within a congregation. What this means is that Covenant Discipleship must not be offered as just another program from which to pick and choose, but rather as a means for providing direction and leadership that will in turn strengthen all the ministries of a congregation.

If you are considering joining a Covenant Discipleship Group, or if you have made that decision and are now participating in such a group, you are part of a growing network of congregations that find this form of mutual accountability to be a source of great strength. As you hold yourself accountable for your discipleship week by week, you will be joining thousands of faithful church members who are responding to the call of Jesus Christ to become more reliable and dependable in their walk with Christ. All of this you will discover as your daily walk with Christ becomes more consistent in the months and years ahead, and as your Covenant Discipleship Group becomes a means of grace through which God empowers you to live out your discipleship in the world with new energy and dedication. The privilege and the assurance of being in covenant with God brings with it a new sense of God's mission and ministry for the church that you can share with the other members of your congregation.

Christian Discipleship: A Matter of Heart and Life

Christian discipleship has been defined as walking with Christ in the world. For John Wesley, this walk was a matter of heart and life. Discipleship is first concerned with what we believe, with our relationship with Jesus Christ. When we believe in Christ, we open our hearts and minds to follow his teachings, and our faithful obedience is proof of our love for him.

In addition to relationship, Jesus said clearly that discipleship involves our daily, and often costly, walk. Some people will thank us for our Christian witness and respond with kindness. Others will not only reject the gospel, they will also hate and despise us. Therefore, we must never measure the effectiveness of our discipleship by how other people respond to the gospel or to our witness. The measure of our discipleship and our love for Jesus must always be our obedience to him and to his teachings.

Spiritual Formation: What We Believe

Christian discipleship begins with acknowledging Jesus Christ as Savior of the world. But faithful discipleship also means being honest about the world we live in, as well as the people with whom we live. Although humans were created in God's own image, we quickly turned away from God into self-sufficiency and idolatry, a condition called sin. This sinfulness requires the radical healing that only God in Jesus Christ can provide.

Our relationship with Christ, which brings us forgiveness from sin and reconciliation with God, is a new life, a spiritual life that came about through God's saving work of grace in Jesus Christ. John Wesley understood the spiritual life to be similar to the natural biological life. Spiritually, our mother is the church, and individual congregations are God's spiritual wombs, entrusted with new lives that are constantly being conceived by the Holy Spirit. These new spiritual lives must be nurtured and cared for, surrounded by the safety and security of a community of faith that provides everything necessary to prepare for the moment when a new spiritual life is brought into the world.

John Wesley's image is powerful: a baby in the womb is in the world but not of the world. A person being nurtured toward spiritual birth in the womb of the church is also very much alive. Moreover, while there is indeed a radical change from womb to world, the change is not a total transformation. The day before a baby is born, it is fully formed in the womb. Likewise, while our spiritual birth is a radical change in our condition, much prior spiritual formation has already taken place. Yet, how often is a congregation aware of the spiritual lives being nurtured toward spiritual birth? And when did a congregation last labor over a spiritual birth?

A phrase often used for spiritual birth is *born again*. Here too the similarities with natural birth are striking. Just as no two natural births are alike, no two spiritual births are alike. Some are relatively quick and easy; others relatively long and laborious. And all births demand much more of the mother than the child. The one constant in it all is that spiritual life begins with God's prevenient grace. *Prevenient grace* is a theological term that describes

Whoever does not carry the cross and follow me cannot be my disciple.

(Luke 14:27)

Now by this we may be sure that we know him, if we obey his commandments. Whoever says, "I have come to know him," but does not obey his commandments, is a liar, . . . whoever says, "I abide in him," ought to walk just as he walked.

(1 John 2:3-6)

God's divine initiative that invites us to forgiveness and reconciliation, gradually wearing down our self-sufficiency, our sinful resistance to grace.

Prevenient grace gives us not only the freedom to resist grace but also the will and desire to make our ultimate surrender to God's justifying grace. Our justification before God is essentially a new relationship with God in which the human will finally submits to the indwelling Holy Spirit and a new spiritual life begins for the forgiven and reconciled child of God.

The parallels between spiritual life and natural life continue in the growth that follows new birth. A baby cannot remain a baby. Either it will live and grow to adulthood or it will die. But while the immediate change brought about through our justification is a new relationship with God, we sustain this new relationship through grace upon grace, a transformation known as sanctification.

Sanctifying grace changes the forgiven sinner from someone who instinctively resists God's presence to someone who instinctively seeks God's presence. As with the natural life, this is a gradual transformation and follows the spiritual birth in Christ just as physical, emotional, and intellectual growth follows the birth of a baby.

Following conception, birth, and growth is maturity, as necessary a part of the spiritual life as it is of the natural life. In the Methodist tradition, this next stage is known as Christian perfection. Since this phrase is often misunderstood, we will speak instead about Christian maturity.

Mature Christian disciples have a sense of growth in the spiritual life that comes from learning and consistently following the teachings of Jesus. However, those of us who have reached maturity in the natural life know that it is nothing to boast about. We still make mistakes, and we are certainly not perfect role models. But we have become seasoned, and the seasoned Christian is a reliable and dependable disciple.

The Christian does not reach maturity quickly or easily. Learning the craft of discipleship takes years of practice, but we have the assurance along the way that our spiritual lives are enfolded by God's prevenient, justifying, and sanctifying grace. And since God's grace is infinitely courteous and never forced, we always have the freedom to resist, growing in grace only to the extent that we exercise our God-given responsibility to do so.

This means accepting the teachings of Jesus as both the guidelines for our spiritual journey and the rules for living in God's household. It also means learning how to practice the rules, regularly and consistently. This process of maturing in the faith is known as Christian formation.

Christian Formation: How We Live

Our relationship with God in Christ can be sustained only by walking with Christ in the world. This means following his teachings and example and making discipleship the focal point of our Christian life. Christian formation, the process of learning how to follow the teachings of Jesus, takes many years of practice. The faithfulness with which early Methodists applied themselves to this task earned them their original nickname, *methodists*.

In forming Christian disciples it is important not to minimize or overlook the relational aspect of the spiritual life, since it is in relationship that we receive the grace and the power to walk with Christ in the world. Without this relationship, the teachings of Jesus become hollow and legalistic, mere rules and regulations that set impossibly high standards.

It is equally important, however, to stress that our spiritual relationship with God is fraught with dishonesty and self-deception if we do not make every effort to do what Jesus said we should do. The teachings of Jesus are summarized in two great commandments: "'You shall love the Lord your God with all your heart, and with all your soul, and with all your mind.' This is the greatest and first commandment. And a second is like it: 'You shall love your neighbor as yourself.' On these two commandments hang all the law and the prophets" (Matthew 22:37-40).

The church has traditionally applied these commandments through two basic principles of discipleship: what we must do to open ourselves to God's grace, and what we must do to share God's grace with the world.

Throughout Christian history these principles have often been described as works of piety and works of mercy, and both are equally necessary for Christian discipleship. Congregations that emphasize both of these principles become vital communities of faithful disciples by leading people to belief in Jesus Christ and then showing them how to walk with him in the power of the Holy Spirit. A community of faith that holds faith and works in a healthy tension becomes a sign of the coming reign of God, a community where God's love, justice, and power are embodied in a foretaste of the kingdom that shall have no end (see Isaiah 9:7).

Methodical Discipleship: The General Rules

Early Methodists developed a way of life that fostered reliability in following these commandments, and their methodical discipleship is best expressed in John Wesley's "The Nature, Design, and General Rules of Our United Societies," or the General Rules, as they came to be known.

Even though these guidelines were first published more than 250 years ago, there is little in them that cannot be easily applied to life in this century. The General Rules state clearly that genuine discipleship is rooted in living out the faith, and the only thing needed is to have both the will and the commitment to discipleship.

An abbreviated version of the General Rules can be found on page 48 of *The Book of Discipline of The United Methodist Church—2000*, and the full text on pages 71–74. The format is quite simple. After a short preamble explaining the nature and purpose of Methodist societies, the Rules deal first with works of mercy that are embodied in Christian tradition.

In the General Rules, Methodists are instructed to do "no harm, by avoiding evil of every kind, especially that which is most generally practiced," and to do good "by being in every kind merciful" and "doing good of every possible sort, and, as far as possible, to all . . ." By first addressing works of mercy, Wesley emphasized that Methodists must take care of people's physical needs first, giving food to the hungry, clothes to the needy, and caring for those who were sick or in prison (Matthew 25:35-36). Only then were they to minister to spiritual needs.

Wesley also cautioned against the false teaching that good works should always be done with a generous spirit. He knew from his own years of rigorous spiritual learning that spiritual promptings can easily be ignored or misinterpreted due to ill temper or lazy disposition. Works of mercy are a primary obligation and responsibility for Christian disciples, even when we are not in the mood.

After works of mercy, the General Rules moved to works of piety, those essential spiritual disciplines for faithful discipleship. Early Methodists were required to attend "upon all the ordinances of God," including public worship; the ministry of the Word, either read or preached; the Lord's Supper; family and private prayer; Bible study; and fasting.

Wesley gave a more detailed description of works of piety in "Minutes of Several Conversations Between the Rev. Mr. Wesley and Others, From the Year 1744, to the Year 1789," pages 322–324, listing them as the instituted means of grace (the basic requirements of the church) and the prudential means of grace (those disciplines and practices that, while not required at all times and in all places, can greatly enhance our spiritual growth).

Instituted means of grace are those listed above, with the addition of Christian conference, defined as right conversation between the people of God, "seasoned with salt," always with "a determinate end in view," and with prayer before and after.

Prudential means of grace are those "particular rules" that help Christians in the "arts of holy living." The more we use these prudential means of grace, the more we will grow in grace. Examples of these are class and band meetings; a steady watch, as Wesley described, "against the world, the devil, yourselves, your besetting sin"; self-denial and temperance in all things; proper dietary habits; and bearing our cross cheerfully as a gift from God.

Perhaps the most significant word throughout the General Rules is Wesley's description of these disciplines as works: *works* of mercy and *works* of piety. The clear implication is that by doing these things, we open ourselves to grace. We do not earn God's grace by doing them. But with the responsibility and obligation given to us by God's grace, we can so order our lives that we are more receptive and more open to grace.

In this sense, works of mercy are as much a channel of grace as works of piety. Not only are they a means of grace to strengthen our faith, but if we neglect them we weaken our relationship with Christ. To sustain our faith, we must not merely talk with Jesus; we must walk with him, which means holding in balance the two great commandments to love God and neighbor.

The importance of Wesley's General Rules is the balance they maintain between all the teachings of Jesus. By adapting and modernizing the language, we can formulate a General Rule of Discipleship that speaks clearly for today's church. However, to make the General Rules accessible, we must first find words that convey to modern Christians the same aspects of servant ministry that mercy and piety conveyed in the eighteenth century. We must also acknowledge that we live in a world that makes a clear distinction between social and personal principles, as well as public and private life; and that such a distinction brings with it an opportunity for greater insights into the significance of these different dimensions of Jesus' commandments.

Two modern phrases that convey the meaning of works of mercy are *acts*

Whoever says, "I have come to know him," but does not obey his commandments, is a liar, and in such a person the truth does not exist; but whoever obeys his word, truly in this person the love of God has reached perfection. By this we may be sure that we are in him: whoever says, "I abide in him," ought to walk just as he walked. (1 John 2:4-6) *of compassion* and *acts of justice*. Two phrases that convey the meaning of works of piety are *acts of devotion* and *acts of worship*. Together they provide the same balanced approach to Christian discipleship that the early Methodists practiced, and offer important guidance for daily Christian living.

A General Rule of Discipleship for the Church of Today

Covenant Discipleship Groups have taken the General Rules of John Wesley and created a General Rule of Discipleship that summarizes the basics of Christian living (see sidebar). Because it is a general rule, it allows for maximum flexibility in its application. Private and personal aspects of discipleship are described as acts of devotion and compassion. Public and social aspects of discipleship are lived out in acts of worship and justice.

Christian witness is the bedrock of our identity as the church, the great privilege as well as the unique responsibility of the Christian life. The General Rule begins with a clear commitment to witness in the world to the Christ whose teachings we endeavor to follow. Many of these teachings are not unique to Jesus. Christians make them unique by declaring who Jesus is and what he taught.

It may seem redundant to add the phrase *in the world* to the opening directive of the General Rule. Surely any witness to Jesus Christ will be in the world, since that is where we live out our discipleship most of the time. This may have been true in eighteenth-century England, but many things have changed since that time.

In the past 250 years, Methodism has become established as a church with thousands of local congregations. Although it is still the practice in many parts of the worldwide church to witness to Jesus Christ, proclaiming him as prophet and redeemer and calling on all people to acknowledge him as sovereign of the coming reign of God, this is seldom a valid assumption in the North American church, where Christian witness is frequently displaced by programs and activities that do everything except give honor to the Christ for whom the church exists.

Concern for programs and buildings in North American congregations has meant that a considerable amount of time and energy is expended in making them attractive enough to entice others to join. The result is that many Christians have neither the time nor the desire to witness to Christ in the world, choosing to witness instead to one another, if they witness at all.

The General Rule first directs dependable Christian disciples to reach out beyond their church communities and let all the world know the good news of the gospel of Jesus Christ. It then instructs Christians to follow the teachings of Jesus through acts of compassion, justice, worship, and devotion. In dealing with each of these areas in turn, we will note that the purpose of the General Rule is to hold us accountable for our walk with Christ.

Acts of Compassion

Acts of compassion are what John Wesley called works of mercy. They are the simple things we do out of kindness to our neighbor, often without giving them much thought. In his General Rules, Wesley listed these before

The General Rule of Discipleship:

To witness to Jesus Christ in the world, and to follow his teachings through acts of compassion, justice, worship, and devotion, under the guidance of the Holy Spirit.

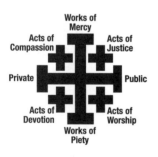

Works of Mercy

Acts of Compassion — Acts of Justice

Private — Public

Acts of Devotion — Acts of Worship

Works of Piety

works of piety. Early Methodists understood that although our faith experience often varies with temperament, circumstance, and mood, service for Christ should not be subject to such variables. The hungry need to be fed, the naked need to be clothed, and the sick need to be visited whether or not it is convenient for us. Those in prison need to be visited whether or not we feel we have much to offer them. Basic acts of compassion can and should be performed by Christian disciples at every opportunity, which is why they are listed as the first of Christ's teachings in the General Rule. All too often those of us with a strong faith experience neglect to incorporate basic acts of compassion into our daily living, only to find these very acts performed on a regular basis by those who are uncomfortable talking about their faith.

This directive of the General Rule makes the balance of faith and works unavoidable for the dependable Christian disciple. Walking with Christ requires us to look around, find out who is in need, and do something about it.

Acts of Justice

Once we do look around and discover needs, the General Rule points us toward another important dimension of Christian discipleship: acts of justice, those ways in which we not only minister to people in need but also ask why they are in need. This is the area in which many faithful disciples are rusty, to say the least. Yet to neglect this aspect of our walk with Christ indicates a profound misunderstanding of his teachings. Jesus was steeped in the Hebrew Scriptures, where divine righteousness and justice are no less powerful than divine love.

God's justice is not a legalistic righteousness, but neither is it an impartial righteousness. Contrary to the Greek and Roman concepts of morality and law that are often inferred from the language of the New Testament, the righteousness of God in the teachings of Jesus has a strongly personal quality and echoes the Old Testament prophets such as Amos, Hosea, and Micah. Most important of all, it is weighted toward the poor and the helpless.

The justice of God is justice with an agenda, the agenda of a God who is deeply offended by those who exercise power irresponsibly. It is the same agenda that Jesus announced in the Nazareth synagogue when he read from the scroll (Isaiah 61:1-2; Luke 4:18-19), and that is affirmed in the Sermon on the Mount. The teachings of Jesus did not abolish the law and the prophets but rather fulfilled them (Matthew 5:17). Disciples of Jesus must do no less.

The General Rule directs us not only to meet people's needs but also to ask why they are in need in the first place. Some of this will happen as a matter of course; for once we get involved with acts of compassion, we will see with new eyes the struggles of the poor and needy. As we recognize aspects of our social and economic systems that are an offense to the God whose law was thundered from Sinai, we will be compelled to join with these people in their struggles, no longer content to remain uninvolved.

This involvement may require us to take stands that are controversial. We know how to minister to hungry people as an act of compassion. It is much less clear what we should do to address the reasons for their hunger. Almost always there are different points of view and many ways of proceeding. And there is no guarantee that we will always be right in this dimension of our discipleship.

These different points of view and ways of proceeding mean that while agreement on particular acts of justice may not be possible, it is important to hold each other accountable for doing something to implement God's justice in the world. One example of such a justice issue in the United States today would be the death penalty. Those who oppose the death penalty can be held accountable for getting involved in ministries with prisoners on death row. Those who support it can be held accountable for ministering to victims of violent crimes. The important thing is to do something rather than merely hold opinions.

Acts of Worship

Acts of worship are the means of grace that we exercise together publicly: the ministries of Word and sacrament that enable us to build each other up in the body of Christ in order to benefit from our mutual gifts and graces. In John Wesley's General Rules, these communal means of grace precede those that are personal. Public worship comes before the disciplines of private prayer, searching the Scriptures, and fasting, or abstinence.

Apart from the fact that this affirms the indispensable place of the church in Christian discipleship, it is yet one more example of the common sense of early Methodists. Our private devotions will often founder on our doubts and uncertainties. When we worship together, however, we "watch over one another in love" and "build each other up" in the body of Christ.

Living as we do at a time of rich liturgical renewal, we have a tremendous advantage when participating in public worship today. Movements such as The Order of Saint Luke are providing innovative leadership. *The United Methodist Hymnal* is one of a number of resources combining new and old riches of Christian tradition. The sacraments are being given renewed prominence as a true means of grace. Contemporary forms of worship are reaching large numbers of people previously disinterested in the faith. And, most important of all, congregations are finding worship to be the time when Christ can be truly honored.

Yet the General Rule has a word of caution at this point. Yes, it is good that the liturgical and sacramental life of the church is being renewed, and that our congregations are increasingly centered on worship as the means of grace that reaches most of our people. But accountable discipleship does not measure the effectiveness of worship merely by the ways in which it addresses the needs of those who participate.

The main reason Christians participate in acts of worship is to glorify God and open ourselves to God's grace. The focus of our worship, both in Word and sacrament, is far more important than the benefits we might derive from it. When we come together as a worshiping community, we enter into sacred time and space that is a true foretaste of eternity. We tread on holy ground and lose ourselves in the presence of God. As with so much else in our discipleship, it is a case of being clear about priorities and obligations of reliable, dependable disciples.

What should we do to honor God? Consider the frequency of Holy Communion as well as the faithfulness at Sunday services. Seek opportunities for worship on days other than Sunday, remembering that two or three gathered in the name of Christ are honored by his presence no less than at the larger worship services.

Acts of Devotion

In many ways, acts of devotion—the private spiritual disciplines of prayer, Bible reading, fasting, and inward examination that bring us face to face with God—are the most demanding part of the General Rule, since it is during these times that we most directly enter into the presence of God. We may well have encountered God in our acts of compassion among homeless, abused, and rejected castoffs of society. We may well have joined with the prophet from Nazareth in our acts of justice, confronting the powers and principalities of this world in the name of the God of righteousness. We may even have encountered the risen Christ through the indwelling Holy Spirit in our acts of worship. Nevertheless, for most of us the times when we come face to face with God most directly are in the disciplines of private devotion, when no one else is present and our conversation with God is intensely personal.

The other dimensions of the General Rule are by no means irrelevant to our acts of devotion, because they insure that we do not make ourselves the center of our life with Christ. But we must never allow them to substitute for private devotions. Self-deception is a very real possibility in the busyness of compassion, justice, and worship. If these activities deprive us of our personal relationship with God, then our discipleship is seriously out of balance.

We must not be overwhelmed by the sense of the holy that surrounds our devotional disciplines. Nor do we need to attempt these acts of devotion in a vacuum. In addition to a wealth of literature on prayer, numerous aids for personal Bible study, and many devotional guides, we have as our role model Jesus of Nazareth and as our mentors that "great . . . cloud of witnesses" who have run their race and are now cheering us on (Hebrews 12:1).

But even with all these resources, we are the ones responsible for developing disciplines of prayer, Bible study, and personal reflection that will ultimately refine us as Christian disciples. It is in those moments of quietness, with nothing to distract and nowhere to hide, that God will deal with us most personally and shape our discipleship most directly.

Promptings and Warnings

When we have begun to exercise accountability for acts of compassion, justice, worship, and devotion, the General Rule calls us to be accountable for another vital aspect of Christian discipleship: obedience to the promptings and warnings of the Holy Spirit. Whenever we meet together in the name of Christ, we watch over one another in love, fully aware that the Spirit of God is present to empower us for our walk with Christ.

This is not only a scriptural promise that Christ will be in the midst of those who gather in his name; it is also something of a warning. Christ will

Whenever we meet together in the name of Christ, we watch over one another in love, fully aware that the Spirit of God is present to empower us for our walk with Christ.

be present on those occasions, and the Holy Spirit will have promptings and warnings for which faithful disciples must be prepared and ready to obey.

Learning how to recognize these spiritual promptings and warnings is one of the most important rewards of a mutually accountable discipleship. To a great extent, it often means simply using the right language. For example, Christian disciples do not have "bright ideas." Rather, they receive promptings or nudges from the Holy Spirit. "Twinges of conscience" are warnings from the Holy Spirit.

Identifying these warnings and promptings sharpens our spiritual discernment. While there is a risk of self-deception when we rely solely on these spiritual intuitions for our discipleship, sharing them with trusted Christian friends and colleagues is a major step forward in the spiritual life because it greatly increases our level of discernment.

Since this is the area in which we are most likely to experience contrasting gifts and graces, this aspect of discipleship offers perhaps the best example of the importance of mutual accountability. We need both spirit and structure to remain accountable for recognizing and obeying the promptings and warnings of the Holy Spirit to do or say particular things at particular times, or to refrain from particular words and deeds.

Some Christians find spiritual promptings and warnings very familiar and readily recognizable. Others will be wary of using spiritual language to describe what they have always regarded as the ordinary experiences of life. However, learning to accept "bright ideas" or "twinges of conscience" as promptings or warnings of the Holy Spirit is precisely what makes the Christian journey so exciting. The ordinary things of life take on new meaning as we come to understand that everything, even the mundane, is a spiritual work of grace.

The Challenge of Christian Discipleship

At this point you might be saying: "Well and good. I can agree with all of the above. But being a Christian disciple is hard. I know I'm going to fall short in following Jesus' teachings, so I'd prefer not to set myself up for failure. I'll just settle for being an ordinary church member: attend worship, play my part, and pull my weight. This discipleship business is too much for me."

The problem with this kind of reaction is that you and I are not exercising an option when we become Christian disciples. We can choose to say yes or no to Jesus, but the reality of Christian discipleship is that it is not our initiative. We do not choose to be disciples of Jesus Christ. He chooses us. And he usually catches us unawares.

We begin the Christian life by accepting the gift of God's salvation, experiencing God's forgiveness and reconciliation, and coming to know the deep joy and inward peace of walking with Christ day by day. Through the indwelling of the Holy Spirit, we are assured of guidance and strength every step of the way as we learn more about the obligations of Christian life. No part of our lives is too small to place in the hands of God as we seek to do the work assigned to us in God's household.

But then we receive a call from Jesus that requires a more intensive relationship and a more demanding walk. The call is to become one of his disciples, and while the invitation leaves nothing in doubt, it leaves everything open. There is only one condition to this call, but it is unconditional: Jesus asks for our trusting obedience in responding to his invitation.

"Follow me," he said to Simon, Andrew, James, and John (Matthew 4:18-22). No probation. No trial period to see if they liked it. No discussion about potential benefits. The reward of following Jesus would be nothing more nor less than the privilege of sharing in his work of servant ministry in the world.

Eventually Jesus' disciples came to realize that the work itself was the richest of rewards, but that could not be their motive for answering the call. The decision to become a disciple of Jesus of Nazareth involved two things: taking an unqualified risk and being willing to abandon everything the world holds dear for the sake of those things that were of eternal importance. Jesus' parables and teachings made that clear time and again: the hidden treasure (Matthew 13:44); the man who built bigger barns (Luke 12:13-21); the prodigal son (Luke 15:11-32); and the harsh directive that being his disciple could mean neglecting one's family and friends (Luke 14:26).

To walk with Jesus as his disciple meant sharing his vision of a new age for this planet, and the conviction that Jesus was the one who would bring it to pass. Jesus' described this vision as the Kingdom, a time when the will of God will be done "on earth as it is in heaven" (Matthew 6:10); a new age, when God will be truly acknowledged by all people, "from the least of them to the greatest" (Jeremiah 31:34); a time when "the wolf shall live with the lamb, the leopard shall lie down with the kid, . . . the lion shall eat straw like the ox," and "the earth will be full of the knowledge of the LORD as the waters cover the sea" (Isaiah 11:6-9); a time of bringing "good news to the poor," "release to the captives," "sight to the blind," and liberty to the oppressed (Luke 4:18-19); a time when there will be neither Jew nor Greek, neither slave nor free, neither male nor female (Galatians 3:28). And now was the time to expect the fulfillment of all these promises. The vision of the Hebrew prophets had become a present reality in the person of Jesus Christ (Luke 4:21).

We know that this vision of the Kingdom led to Jesus' horrible and agonizing death on the cross. We also know that many of his followers across the centuries have given their lives in his service. This century is no exception, and the stories of martyrdom come to us with disturbing regularity.

For many of us, this makes the call to discipleship a real dilemma. We try to maintain a faithful witness in our life and work, but we are only too aware that our Christian discipleship cost is very little and that rarely is one of our lives in danger. Our problems are more likely to be the subtle grip of affluence, even when our share of it is quite modest. We are so consumed with meeting the challenges of each new day that we seem to have no energy—physical, emotional, intellectual, or spiritual—to face a more challenging discipleship.

Yet the call of Christ persists. "Follow me! I need your help if my vision

The decision to become a disciple of Jesus of Nazareth involved taking an unqualified risk and being willing to abandon everything the world holds dear for the sake of those things that were of eternal importance.

I do not understand my own actions. For I do not do what I want, but I do the very thing I hate. Now if I do what I do not want, I agree that the law is good. But in fact it is no longer I that do it, but sin that dwells within me. . . . For I delight in the law of God in my inmost self, but I see in my members another law at war with the law of my mind, making me captive to the law of sin that dwells in my members. Wretched man that I am! Who will rescue me from this body of death?

(Romans 7:15-19, 22-24)

is to be fulfilled. I need to know if you are dependable, if I can rely on you and trust you. Will you be my disciple?" How are we to answer this call from a Jesus who seems to be striding ahead of us?

Such persistence sends us back to the Scriptures with renewed urgency, and we are relieved to find that our dilemma is not new. As Paul makes clear in his letter to the church at Rome, when we hear the call of Christ to a deeper commitment, the grace of our salvation strikes us with a new and critical self-awareness, in response to which there first comes a new repentance and then a sense of release. Our new and more profound repentance enables us to feel the depth of Paul's remorse and to see with new insight the true extent of the sin Paul writes about in Romans 7. Then comes a new sense of release as we experience more profoundly the depths of our forgiveness and reconciliation in Christ.

The great good news of the gospel is the declaration by God in Christ that in spite of our sin, in spite of our imperfections, we are accepted by God just as we are, no longer measured by what we know we ought to do, nor by what others do, nor by what others tell us we ought to do. The good news of the gospel is the assurance that when we do the best we can to follow Jesus Christ, that is good enough for God.

We are freed from all burdens because we know that we are reconciled as members of God's family. Whatever our level of accomplishment and commitment, we have the deep joy and peace of knowing that we are in tune with the eternal. Mistakes and shortcomings remain, but there is no compromise of intent, since nothing can hold us back from seeking to serve Christ boldly and unreservedly.

Just as the inviting power of grace awakens us to repentance, the reconciling power of grace restores us to God's love. All of this we see with the more revealing illumination of Christian discipleship once we have made the commitment to follow Jesus Christ more reliably and dependably in deed as well as word. For once we accept the condition of unconditional obedience to Christ, we are honored by the Holy Spirit with profound new insights into the work of God in the world. Having made this further commitment to Christ, we are trusted with more information about the purpose of our call, and given more power for the task at hand.

What was true for the first disciples is also true for us today. Jesus promises us the privilege of his friendship as he challenges us to become his disciples in preparing for God's salvation of the world. This is an offer of true friendship, a sharing of everything. As such, it is a friendship that works both ways. Not only are we entrusted with deeper insights into our sin and salvation, but we are also expected to join Christ more directly and sympathetically in the suffering and injustice of the world.

As Paul goes on to say in Romans, we are heirs with Christ, provided we suffer with him in order that we might be glorified with him. Christ's victory over sin is not yet here in its fullness, and those who accept his call to discipleship must be ready for a struggle, not only with their own sin but also with the resistance of a sinful world.

This is a sobering word, and yet the vision leaves us breathless in awe and wonder. Our call to discipleship introduces us to the global, even cosmic, scope of God's plan of salvation. Just as we have been given new life through our reconciliation with God in Christ, so God intends new life for the whole of creation. Just as our own rebirth comes through the labor and suffering of Jesus Christ, so does that of the world. As disciples of Jesus Christ we are called to share in that labor and suffering.

We find that the world is God's sphere of salvation, and that disciples must join him where he is at work. We have received forgiveness and reconciliation in Christ, but now our call to discipleship sends us into a world where we are confronted very directly with sin, suffering, and evil that are not just personal but global and systemic. Christ now calls us beyond the joy and the freedom of personal salvation into a discipleship that shares his burdens, on our doorstep and around the world.

The question therefore becomes how to be obedient to Christ more dependably and reliably. How are we to become more trustworthy disciples now that Christ has entrusted us with so much more. And how are we to do this in a world that remains rebellious against God, and knowing furthermore that we still find rebellious tendencies in ourselves?

The dilemma of Romans 7 seems to return with even greater tension, and even anguish. Once again we find the answer in the heritage of early Methodism, since a key element in Wesley's teaching on prevenient grace is that God's grace will always offer the freedom to resist grace. Thus, our new relationship with God is a continual choice. If the relationship is to be sustained, it must be worked out in the world through an obedient discipleship. If the choice is disobedience, however, then the new relationship can be broken. If broken habitually, it can even be destroyed.

Wesley's point was not that obedient discipleship is necessary to earn our new relationship with God in Christ, but rather that obedient discipleship is necessary to sustain that new relationship. Following the teachings of Jesus is not the precondition of salvation but the post-condition—the necessity that those who are now part of God's household must obey the house rules.

This necessity of obedience was a revolutionary teaching in Wesley's day, and it is no less revolutionary today. Properly taught and applied, it could turn our congregations into the Christ-centered communities of faith we always hope they will be. This necessity of obedience is also at the heart of the question put to ordinands in the Methodist tradition ever since the days of Wesley: "Are you going on to perfection?" This does not mean a sinless perfection but a maturity of consistent obedience to Christ, in which the human will loses its tendency to resist God's grace. The critical question for Christian disciples, therefore, is how to permit God's grace to foster a maturity of constant obedience so that the person's service for Christ in the world might work with unimpeded grace, power, and love.

Wesley's theological understanding of this question led him to adopt what first seemed an unbelievably straightforward solution: a weekly meeting of like-minded people to exercise a mutual accountability for their discipleship. These class meetings became a prudential means of grace, as profound as they were simple. In adopting class meetings as the basic format of early Methodism, Wesley was not only being practical but was also drawing on the cardinal principle of grace: Authentic Christian

There is therefore now no condemnation for those who are in Christ Jesus. For the law of the Spirit of life in Christ Jesus has set you free from the law of sin and of death. For God has done what the law, weakened by the flesh, could not do: by sending his own Son in the likeness of sinful flesh, and to deal with sin, he condemned sin in the flesh, so that the just requirement of the law might be fulfilled in us, who walk not according to the flesh but according to the Spirit. (Romans 8:1-4)

I consider that the sufferings of this present time are not worth comparing with the glory about to be revealed to us. For the creation waits with eager longing for the revealing of the children of God; . . . in hope that the creation itself will be set free from its bondage to decay and will obtain the freedom of the glory of the children of God. . . . For in hope we were saved. Now hope that is seen is not hope. For who hopes for what is seen? But if we hope for what we do not see, we wait for it with patience.

(Romans 8:18-25)

discipleship consists of learning how to say yes to God and holding one another accountable for so doing. It remains the most significant contribution made by the early Methodists to the church of their day, and ours.

The key to understanding the dynamic of the early class meeting is the mutual accountability exercised by its members. They developed an openness to, and a trust of, one another that permitted them to share their spiritual pilgrimage. But we must not assume that the class meeting was what we would call today an intensive group experience. While Wesley said that the purpose of these weekly meetings was to "watch over one another in love," we misunderstand their nature and purpose if we emphasize the love that was shared between the members to the neglect of the mutual accountability that strengthened their obedience to Christ.

This simple and straightforward method affirmed that although people may respond to God's grace with varying degrees of acceptance or resistance, the teachings of Christ are so basic that, through the grace of God, they can be attempted by anyone who has the desire to do so. Likewise, there are basic spiritual disciplines through which all can receive God's grace if they are willing to open themselves. Whatever our religious experience, and whatever our degree of faith, we can do our best to be obedient disciples and know that our efforts will be acceptable to God.

The distinctive quality of early Methodists' discipleship was that Christians held themselves accountable for their obedience to Christ. Through Christian fellowship and community, they helped one another grow in grace, but their priority was to develop a consistent obedience to Jesus Christ. Their commitment to mutual accountability expressed belief in a redemption that gave freedom under God's grace, but that also gave responsibility. In short, they worked out their salvation.

The weekly class meeting proved to be the most reliable way of doing this. It was a supportive structure for discipleship, grounded in the realities of daily living in the world and undergirded by common sense that proved to be the binding muscle of the early Methodist movement, giving it both strength and resilience. Early Methodists did not seek God in their class meetings, since they knew that God had found them right where they lived and worked. Instead, it was their mutual accountability week by week that gave them the grace to see Jesus Christ in the world and the strength to join him.

In 1749, Charles Wesley wrote a hymn for Methodists to sing on their way to work after listening to early morning preaching at 5:00 A.M. The words to that hymn still convey the spiritual power of these spiritual giants:

> Forth in thy name, O Lord, I go,
> my daily labor to pursue;
> thee, only thee, resolved to know
> in all I think or speak or do.
>
> The task thy wisdom hath assigned,
> O let me cheerfully fulfill;
> in all my works thy presence find,
> and prove thy good and perfect will.

Part
2

What Are Covenant Discipleship Groups?

This is the covenant that I will make with them
    after those days, says the Lord:
I will put my laws in their hearts,
    and I will write them on their minds.
                                    (Hebrews 10:16)

Covenant Discipleship Groups: Class Meetings for Today's Church

If we are to learn from our spiritual forebears, we must do more than simply go back to eighteenth-century England and transfer early Methodist practices into the present century. Instead, we must look at the class meeting in its own setting and see whether such a model of disciplined discipleship can teach us something about our discipleship today, whether a new plant can grow in the soil of a different time and place.

As we look for ways to adapt early Methodist practices to the present time, we must keep in mind that early Methodism was not part of the institutional church. Methodism was a movement within the much larger Church of England, and the great majority of church members did not respond to the call to committed discipleship found in Wesley's General Rules. The United Methodist Church of today faces the same situation.

An important aspect of Covenant Discipleship Groups is that they take place in small groups. Small groups have become a useful and necessary component of our contemporary social fabric, helping to strengthen and sustain the community of faith in all sorts of ways. But if we are to learn from the class meeting, we must be clear that its distinctive dynamic was to provide mutual accountability for the work of discipleship. This foundational dynamic of accountability is quite different from that of most other small groups, which often exist primarily for support, learning, and fellowship.

Joining with people of like mind and purpose in order to make our discipleship more effective is just plain, practical common sense, which explains why this approach is widely used in other walks of life. People who wish to establish an exercise routine for jogging, tennis, or aerobics will find a partner. Fixing a car or a roof or even clearing out a garage is put off indefinitely until we ask a friend to help us.

The clearest example of this practice today is found in Alcoholics Anonymous and similar programs where individuals, faced with a common problem, first acknowledge the problem and then commit to helping one another keep it under control. Although members of these groups never say they have overcome the problem, they can reach a point where resisting it is possible by living one day at a time.

Christian discipleship is much the same. Our problem is that we are sinners and will continue to be sinners until our salvation in Christ has been brought to the fullness of God's reign on earth as in heaven. We know we are forgiven and reconciled sinners, accepted by the grace of God just as we are. But we also know that our new relationship with God requires us to grow in grace "until all of us come to the unity of the faith and of the knowledge of the Son of God, to maturity, to the measure of the full stature of Christ" (Ephesians 4:13). There is no standing still. If we fail to grow in grace, we lose our new relationship.

When we first come to Christ, the joy and the peace of our forgiveness and reconciliation with God is so overwhelming that we often fail to see the need for mutual accountability. However, the longer we walk with Christ the more we realize that our pilgrimage is just beginning, and that we need strength and support for the journey. It is at this point that Christ calls us to a deeper commitment, bringing our walk with him to a different plane where we must learn how to be a disciplined disciple.

To be a disciplined disciple means that our discipleship will go beyond the basics of service to others, beyond the basics of our devotional life. We will now be called upon to serve those whom Jesus specifically wishes us to serve, at those times and in those places specifically determined by him. Learning this disciplined discipleship will take a lifetime, but the most important lesson we must learn along the way is that discipleship is less about a constant task than it is about being on constant call.

At any time, Jesus may require a particular word of compassion, a particular act of justice, or a particular refusal to act or speak. The reliable, dependable disciple must be ready for his instructions, which usually come as promptings or warnings of the Holy Spirit that direct us to what needs doing or saying at particular times and places. Recognizing these promptings and warnings of the Holy Spirit is a sign of mature discipleship.

The freedom of mature discipleship is that we need not worry about what Christ might ask us to do. The question becomes, What does Christ want us to do right now? For whatever Christ asks us to do will always be accompanied by two clear assurances from the Holy Spirit: We will know that it is unquestionably the right thing to do at the time, and we will be given whatever strength we need to accomplish it. Whenever we find ourselves worrying about what we might need to do for Christ, it is almost always an indication that we are evading a more obvious, and probably quite simple, task that Christ is calling us to do here and now.

However, this more immediate task carries an important proviso. We are free to be the companions of Christ in the world if we exercise the responsibility of following his teachings and opening ourselves to the Holy Spirit. Paul's advice in Romans 12:1-2 is both simple and profound: Allow God's grace to work in our lives, for the grace of God is the only strength through which we can become faithful disciples. The words are not an appeal to self-discipline; neither are they an exhortation to strive for personal or social transformation. However, the advice raises two critical questions: What are we doing to ensure that we are open to God's grace? What are we doing to ensure that we are indeed following the teachings of Jesus?

When Christ calls us to discipleship, these are the questions that will not go away. We turn to our mentors in the faith and find that reliable, dependable discipleship lies not only in repentance, forgiveness, and reconciliation but also in well-tried practices (spiritual disciplines) through which Christians across the centuries have opened themselves to God's grace and followed Christ's teachings. We find that these practices require a disciplined commitment if they are to be means of grace in our lives. If they are not integral to the life and work of congregations, they quickly become peripheral to the mission and ministry of the church.

The common sense of early Methodists is easy to comprehend. If the call of Christ to discipleship does make requirements of us, if these requirements are clearly laid out in the teachings of Jesus, if they can be

I appeal to you therefore, brothers and sisters, by the mercies of God, to present your bodies as a living sacrifice, holy and acceptable to God, which is your spiritual worship. Do not be conformed to this world, but be transformed by the renewing of your minds, so that you may discern what is the will of God— what is good and acceptable and perfect. (Romans 12:1-2) met only by availing ourselves of God's grace and certainly not in our own strength, and if the church has found across the centuries that there are reliable channels for this grace, then good sense must surely dictate that Christians use these means of grace in the fullest possible way and thereby fulfill their obligations to Jesus Christ. If Christ has called us to a dependable discipleship and we are not using these means of grace or meeting our obligations to live out his teachings in the world, then we should be asking ourselves with some urgency, Why not?

One reason for our resistance to accountability is a reluctance to interfere in the discipleship of other people. Yet the importance of role models in the Christian life is unquestioned. While we all have been formed in our discipleship by the example of others, for many these examples are difficult to find today.

Many people have begun to feel that the time has come to move forward boldly and to recover the mutual accountability of our Methodist forebears. If those of us called by Christ were to follow our forebears' example and meet weekly to give each other a compass heading in the Christian life, we might become the role models for reliable, dependable discipleship that the church so badly needs. The weekly accountability of early Methodists made a huge difference in their discipleship. They followed Jesus of Nazareth with integrity, accepted his guidelines for doing the work of God in the world, endeavored to follow the guidelines faithfully in their daily living, and all the while took every opportunity to avail themselves of the means of grace.

The Christian church of today needs to exercise the basic common sense of our spiritual forebears and take the necessary steps to drink deeply, as they did, from the well of the gospel. There are too many shallow ponds enticing us with mere reflections of the gospel. Christ needs seasoned disciples who know the difference. Covenant Discipleship Groups are designed to provide us with a way forward, to empower us to answer the call of Christ to be reliable, dependable disciples.

The Meaning of Covenant

Since *covenant* and *disciple* are two of the most important words in the life and work of the church, it is helpful to define each of them and understand the relationship between them.

The scriptural meaning of *covenant* is to enter willingly into a binding agreement with God. It is a response to God's gracious initiative; and, however difficult it might be to keep, it cannot be adjusted. It can only be broken.

First, there is the covenant that God made with the whole of humankind, the covenant of forgiveness and reconciliation. God assures Noah that this covenant is made "with all flesh that is on the earth" and expresses God's promise never again to destroy the earth (Genesis 9:8-17).

Then there is the covenant that God made with the people of Israel, beginning with Abraham (Genesis 17:1-8). The continuing basis of Israel's relationship with Yahweh is found in the covenant made with Moses and those who followed him out of Egypt (Deuteronomy 5). Entered into freely as a response to God's gracious acts toward the Israelites, this covenant has to be renewed voluntarily by each generation; yet it is not unconditional.

Even though the predominant nature of this covenant is God's grace, and the initiative remains with God, there are commandments to be obeyed. When Israel fails to accept these obligations, it is made clear that they are repudiating their covenant relationship with God (Isaiah 1:2-4; Jeremiah 18:1-17; Hosea 6:7, 8:1). They learn the hard way that there is no greater captivity than to be enslaved to self-interest and self-gratification. The only true freedom is to be bound to God in faithful obedience (Exodus 29:45; Jeremiah 7:22-23).

The covenant with Israel culminates in the promise proclaimed by the prophet Jeremiah:

> The days are surely coming, says the LORD, when I will make a new covenant with the house of Israel and the house of Judah. It will not be like the covenant that I made with their ancestors when I took them by the hand to bring them out of the land of Egypt—a covenant that they broke, though I was their husband, says the LORD. But this is the covenant that I will make with the house of Israel after those days, says the LORD: I will put my law within them, and I will write it on their hearts; and I will be their God, and they shall be my people. No longer shall they teach one another, or say to each other, "Know the LORD," for they shall all know me, from the least of them to the greatest, says the LORD; for I will forgive their iniquity, and remember their sin no more.
>
> Jeremiah 31:31-34

In the New Testament, this becomes the new covenant of the Spirit, mediated through Jesus Christ, who himself fulfilled the law, and in whose service is perfect freedom (Acts 2:14-18; 2 Corinthians 3:7-18; Galatians 5:16-18; Hebrews 9:15). Covenant with God is always a gracious concept in the Old Testament, with a focus on God's love. In the New Testament, however, instead of a righteousness that comes from obedient response to God's covenant initiative, there is now a total dependence on Christ. Obedience is still the condition of the covenant relationship, but it is Christ who brings the people of God into a new covenant. It is Christ who sustains them in their righteousness. It is being one with Christ that affords death to sin and the promise of resurrection.

The new covenant is participation in the transformation of the human race, accomplished by Jesus Christ to be fulfilled at his return. This is why the supreme privilege of the Christian is to be called into covenant, into a relationship with the Creator of the universe who invites our help with the unfinished work of the salvation of the world.

Lastly, there are the covenants that Christian disciples make with one another as they endeavor to walk faithfully with Christ. These covenant relationships are likewise at the invitation of Jesus Christ and empowered by the Holy Spirit, but they are very much our responsibility. They are the very foundation of the communities of faith that make up the church, and they are the truest expression of what Paul called the body of Christ (1 Corinthians 12:27).

With all wisdom and insight he has made known to us the mystery of his will, according to his good pleasure that he set forth in Christ, as a plan for the fullness of time, to gather up all things in him, things in heaven and things on earth. (Ephesians 1:8-9)

He himself is before all things, and in him all things hold together. He is the head of the body, the church; he is the beginning, the firstborn from the dead, so that he might come to have first place in everything. For in him all the fullness of God was pleased to dwell, and through him God was pleased to reconcile to himself all things, whether on earth or in heaven, by making peace through the blood of his cross.

(Colossians 1:17-20)

The purpose of these covenants with one another is to make sure that our covenant with Christ is being honored to the best of our ability. Without these human-to-human covenants, we find ourselves attempting to do what no Christian has yet been able to accomplish, namely, go it alone.

There are several things we should note about these various covenants.

1. They are all at God's initiative. Our contribution to all of these covenants is merely to respond to God's initiative. In other words, they are gracious covenants, even the covenants we make with one another; and the Old and New Testaments are altogether clear on this point. No covenant is possible apart from the grace of God (Genesis 6:18; Exodus 6:4; Jeremiah 31:31-34; Hebrews 10:16).

2. God is always faithful in covenant, but we are not. Time and again we read in Scripture that the people of God broke their covenant (Jeremiah 11:10; Hosea 6:7). Those of us in the church today have hardly improved on their performance. Yet in spite of our unfaithfulness, God remains steadfast and patiently waits for us to be more faithful, which is why there must never be any compromise of intent on our part. However inconsistent the Israelites were in fulfilling their obligations, God always honored their every attempt (Psalm 25:10, 103:17-18). The only servant to be dishonored in Jesus' parable about the use of talents was the servant who did nothing with what he had been given but instead buried it in the ground (Matthew 25:30).

3. Covenants are not temporary arrangements. God's covenants are always permanent (Leviticus 24:8; Isaiah 55:3; Hebrews 13:20). The very least we can do is enter into covenant with God unreservedly. The short-term agreements so popular in the church of today—supposedly to entice, persuade, or motivate us into something more permanent as soon as we find it convenient—are a serious compromise and are rarely effective. To be in covenant with God may or may not be convenient, but the relationship is always for our eternal well-being. So-called "short-term covenants" are a contradiction in terms.

4. The covenants we make with one another help us keep our covenant with God. We make covenants with one another because we live in a world that has yet to accept God's salvation. We constantly face temptations to turn away from God, and we need some means of mutual support. John Wesley and the early Methodists understood this need and saw that nothing short of binding themselves to mutual accountability would suffice. By the grace of God, they agreed to "watch over each other in love."

The Meaning of Discipleship

If our covenants with God or with one another are to mean anything at all, we must first do everything in our power to keep them. The word *discipleship* offers the key not only to understanding the word *covenant* but also to empowering us to live as faithful disciples day by day.

Discipleship is the discipline of being in covenant with God. While the grace of God is the primary source for this power, we too have a part to play. We must allow God's grace to work in our lives and accept the conditions by which this can happen.

The origin of the word *disciple* is the Latin word *discipulus*, meaning a student who was willing to make a total commitment in order to learn the mind, as well as the craft, of a particular teacher. The word still means the same today: assuming the closest of bonds and spending a great deal of time with the teacher while furthering the practical implications of his or her teachings.

This sort of relationship explains why Jesus called his disciples to follow him in person. Wherever Jesus went, they went; whatever he did, they tried to do, learning from him as they walked and talked together. In reality, the disciples learned more than they realized, but it was only after Jesus' death and resurrection that they came to understand many of his teachings and his actions.

The only way these original disciples could have learned so much from Jesus was by first sacrificing other priorities, which is precisely what they did. They left their work (Luke 5:11) and they left their families (Matthew 4:18-22). Indeed, as Peter reminded Jesus, they left everything to follow him (Mark 10:28-31). Jesus does not ask everyone, or even every disciple, to make such a complete sacrifice. But the disciple must always be ready to do so if asked.

Christians today use the word *disciple* much more loosely. We tend to apply it to anyone who has come to believe in Jesus Christ, overlooking the fact that belief in Christ does not necessarily make someone a disciplined follower of Christ. Most church members today bear a closer resemblance to the great multitudes of people who followed Jesus, often from a distance and usually in crowds. They listened to his parables and came to be healed and fed, and many of them believed in what he taught. But few accepted the more demanding role of disciple.

It is important to make this distinction between discipleship and church membership. Many church members do not feel the need for mutual accountability. Indeed, some will react defensively to the idea. This should not prevent you from responding to God's call to this greater commitment in your own life. The larger company of your congregation will be enriched through your dependable discipleship, and your leadership in its mission and ministry will be strengthened. These changes will occur gradually through the steady building up of the body as the grace of Christ flows more freely through all the limbs and organs that make up your community of faith.

> But Jesus has now obtained a more excellent ministry, and to that degree he is the mediator of a better covenant, which has been enacted through better promises. For if that first covenant had been faultless, there would have been no need to look for a second one. (Hebrews 8:6-7)

Covenant Discipleship Groups

Now that we have examined the words *covenant* and *discipleship*, we will turn to an examination of Covenant Discipleship Groups themselves by offering several working definitions.

First and foremost, a Covenant Discipleship Group is where Christian disciples give an account of their walk with Christ in a way that enables other members of the group to practice their own discipleship more faithfully.

A Covenant Discipleship Group is open-ended, an ongoing agreement made with God and with the group that is not to be tried and then dropped if it is not immediately or always fulfilling.

A Covenant Discipleship Groups consists of up to seven persons (purely and simply because of time constraints and logistics) who meet together for one hour each week to hold themselves mutually accountable for their discipleship. They do this by means of a covenant that they have written.

A Covenant Discipleship Group is a task-oriented gathering of faithful Christians whose purpose is, first and foremost, to help one another become better disciples of Jesus Christ by watching over one another in love.

A Covenant Discipleship Group is a trustworthy and effective means of identifying and nurturing leaders in discipleship who can help other members of the congregation grow in grace and follow the teachings of Christ.

A Covenant Discipleship Group is a task-oriented gathering of faithful Christians whose purpose is, first and foremost, to help one another become better disciples of Jesus Christ by watching over one another in love.

A Covenant Discipleship Group has no membership restrictions concerning age, gender, or marital status. Most groups have both men and women and frequently have a wide age range as well. The one thing that determines which group a person joins is convenience of schedule.

Having given several working definitions for what Covenant Discipleship Groups are, it is important to state clearly what Covenant Discipleship Groups are not. There are many different types of small groups in the church today. Making the distinction between Covenant Discipleship Groups and other small groups helps clarify the nature and purpose of Covenant Discipleship Groups and can prevent false expectations of what a Covenant Discipleship Group can be expected to accomplish.

Covenant Discipleship Groups are not

- Bible study groups
- Prayer groups
- Encounter groups
- Cell groups
- Spiritual formation groups
- Share groups
- Neighborhood groups
- Service groups
- Advocacy groups
- Growth groups
- Social outreach groups
- Care groups

All of these small groups, and many others, are ways in which Christians can grow in grace, form Christian community, support one another in the Christian life, and deepen their discipleship. In contrast, Covenant Discipleship Groups are intended solely for mutual accountability and prayerful support for living as disciples in the world. They are not where our discipleship happens but where we make sure that it happens.

If there are no Covenant Discipleship Groups in your congregation, there is no reason for you not to form a group. You will obviously need other interested people and a copy of this handbook. However, no other training is required, and there is no enrollment cost.

If the group you form is the first Covenant Discipleship Group in your congregation, then by definition it will be a pilot group, and a pastor of the congregation needs to be in it as a peer member. Since Covenant Discipleship Groups are intended to develop congregational leadership, they will work best if there is pastoral participation at the outset.

We are all on a common journey of discipleship, and ordained clergy need mutual support and accountability for their discipleship no less than laity. Even so, some people feel uncomfortable about having a pastor in their group, even as a peer member. And some pastors are uncomfortable with the idea, rightly concerned that they might find it difficult to be involved in mutual accountability due to the confidences they must keep as part of their pastoral role in the congregation. However, pastors soon discover that the agenda of a Covenant Discipleship Group need not compromise their pastoral relationships.

Pilot groups meet for a year or more to lead a congregation into Covenant Discipleship, and there is no better way to get started than to be part of such a group. Pilot group members discover what is involved firsthand and help form new groups at the end of the pilot year.

At the conclusion of the pilot year, a special weekend is organized to introduce the groups to the whole congregation. The focal point of this weekend is an open invitation during Sunday morning worship. Those who respond are organized into new groups, which begin to meet as soon as days and times can be arranged. Once Covenant Discipleship Groups are part of the congregation, invitations to join can be extended throughout the year, though Covenant Sunday (traditionally one of the Sundays after the Epiphany) is a ready-made occasion.

Prospective members are welcome to attend Covenant Discipleship meetings, either at their own request or by invitation of a member. After three such visits, the prospective member should be asked to make a decision about whether or not to join.

As is the case with any organization or group, members of Covenant Discipleship Groups are expected to make the group meetings an integral part of the weekly schedule. The first and most important priority for members of Covenant Discipleship Groups is regular attendance. In other words, just be there!

Once you have joined a Covenant Discipleship Group, begin right away to arrange your calendar so as to avoid conflicts with this weekly appointment. Think of your attendance at the group as one of your basic routines, something you do as a matter of course unless there is an emergency or you are away from home. It is surprising how seldom you need to be absent once you have made this time a priority.

Surprise absences not only make it difficult for the others to watch over you in love, they also place a burden on the mutual trust of the group. If your absence is unavoidable, let someone know that you cannot be there, and whenever possible try to link up with the group in some way. For example, you may be able to talk by telephone for a few minutes while the group is meeting, or you may be able to pause for prayer at the time the group is meeting. When you return, be ready to give an account of your discipleship for the whole of the time since you were last in attendance.

Regular attendance at group meetings is important for several other reasons. We are in covenant with God in a binding, nonnegotiable agreement that we cannot change or amend, even if it proves to be inconvenient. All we can do is break it. The covenant we make with one another is just as binding as the one we made with God. Our agreement to meet weekly must be kept as faithfully as any other part of our discipleship.

Regular attendance removes pressure and everyone can relax, knowing that the group does not have to prove itself to anyone. No one feels under any obligation to have a group "happening" or to insure that the group meeting is successful or meaningful.

In the midst of so many uncertain human relationships—dishonest promises, broken agreements, family disintegration, demands for instant satisfaction, selfishness masquerading as self-fulfillment—the commitment to be at the weekly meeting is one of the most important gifts that Covenant Discipleship Group members give to one another.

Just as Christ gave us his assurance that when we gather in his name he will be there, so we make this the most important rule of Covenant Discipleship: We too will be there. This commitment imparts to each member a deep sense of comfort and assurance and is in itself a means of grace. The very words *reliable* and *dependable* are music to the ears of pastoral leaders, both clergy and lay.

It is important to understand that our commitment to become part of a Covenant Discipleship Group is a commitment to God and is therefore open-ended; in other words, it does not end. Since we live in a mobile society, the people whom the commitment is made to may not stay the same. People move and schedules change. But as long as you are able to attend the weekly meetings, the other members need the assurance of your commitment.

Because the open-ended nature of the commitment is made clear at the outset, many church members draw back from joining Covenant Discipleship Groups. But by the same token, very few people leave them, because people understand that when they join a Covenant Discipleship Group, they are answering God's call to a more dependable discipleship. Therefore there is only one valid reason for leaving, and that is an equally strong call to be accountable for their discipleship in other ways.

If a member reaches such a decision prayerfully, then departure from the group should be intentional, communicated to the other members at one of the weekly meetings, and implemented with the positive affirmation of the group as a whole. But if a member is merely experiencing discomfort with the process or is questioning the purpose of the group, then his or her feelings should be discussed promptly and candidly. Almost always such an experience signals a growth point for the person as well as for the group.

In our consumeristic culture it is often argued that true freedom of choice requires a number of options, the "multiple choice" that has become such a staple of our educational diet. Yet there is a serious flaw to this argument. In order for multiple choice to be available, someone somewhere has to determine what those choices are. A multiple choice examination usually reveals far more about the teacher than the subject.

By contrast, Christ's invitation to be his disciple does not attempt to manipulate us by claiming to offer options that, their multiplicity notwithstanding, are in fact highly restrictive. Christ offers us a clear choice: the freedom to go our own way with all the enslavement of self-centeredness and self-fulfillment, or the decision to accept the house rules of the kingdom of God with the radical freedom of walking with Christ.

If all of the above seems demanding or legalistic, we must remember the radical freedom Jesus always extended to his disciples. They were always free to leave him; and many of them did, even after performing miracles in his name (Luke 10:17; John 6:66). They were always free to say yes or no.

Adaptations of Covenant Discipleship Groups

While there are no hard and fast rules about the age of Covenant Discipleship Group members, it is often helpful to have peer groups for young people. Youth Covenant Discipleship Groups and Covenant Discipleship Groups for children (often called Sprouts) are Covenant Discipleship Groups that have been adapted to meet the particular life situations of youth and children.

Covenant Discipleship Groups have been formed on college campuses. Covenant Discipleship Groups can also be found at a number of seminaries, divinity schools, and schools of theology, where they are either part of the curriculum or recognized student groups. The groups function in the same way as in congregations, the main difference being that they meet only through the academic year and usually regroup each fall and spring.

Some Common Questions

When people make the decision to join a Covenant Discipleship Group, it is usually because they have heard the call of Christ to become a more dependable disciple, and they want to meet that challenge with commitment and purpose. As with most important steps in the Christian life, however, there are questions to be asked in making the decision, and just as often there are second thoughts when the decision has been made.

If you are wondering whether you should join a Covenant Discipleship Group, or whether you have done the right thing in joining, you need to know that you are not alone. Almost everyone who takes part in Covenant Discipleship has questions about the groups, the covenant, and the process, both before and after they have committed. Here are some of the most common questions and some possible answers.

Why am I joining a Covenant Discipleship Group?

In the first place, Christian discipleship is not a matter of personal choice. It is much more a matter of surrender, a giving-in to God's gracious initiatives in our lives. We may sing the old hymn "Have Thine Own Way, Lord" to express our devotion to Christ. But for those of us who have come to this point of surrender, there really is a note of desperation, much as expressed in the song, when we finally quit resisting God's grace, when we discover that we must hand everything over to God. "Very well, God, have it your way! I can't manage by myself any more."

When we answer the call to discipleship, we respond in blind trust. We are at the end of our tether. We may not yet be sure of our discipleship,

When people make the decision to join a Covenant Discipleship Group, it is usually because they have heard the call of Christ to become a more dependable disciple, and they want to meet that challenge with commitment and purpose.

but we are very sure of Jesus Christ and nothing else, no one else. We do not know where Christ is going to lead us or what he will ask us to do. All we know is that we are now willing to take the risk of following him regardless, because all other options have been closed.

It may be that you have come to this point at an early stage in your Christian pilgrimage. If so, you are blessed indeed; for you have found Christian wisdom much sooner than most of us. More likely, however, you made a commitment to Christ some time ago and have been trying to live a faithful Christian life for many years. So far, so good. You have done your best to be obedient to the teachings of Jesus, and you have sought to walk by the grace of the Holy Spirit.

But now there is another call. Christ becomes candid, even blunt: "Follow me more closely. I have much more for you to learn and to do. I need your disciplined commitment now. Will you take another step with me? Will you trust me even more? And will you let me trust you?"

You have said yes to this call. You are joining a Covenant Discipleship Group so that you can become the dependable disciple Jesus needs.

Does this mean that my discipleship has been inadequate?

Not at all. In fact, quite the contrary or you would not even be hearing this new call. Your discipleship thus far has probably been commendable—witness to Christ at work, at home, and in your neighborhood; regular attendance at church; faithful participation in a Sunday school class; involvement in church activities; regular Bible study; participation in worship and Holy Communion; personal devotions of prayer and meditation—and all have made you a faithful servant of Jesus Christ.

You have likewise been faithful in obeying the commandments of Christ to serve God and your neighbor. Perhaps you have been one of those nameless workers who have visited hospitals, ministered to those in prison, staffed their church's outreach ministries to the poor, and even opened their home to those in need. Or maybe your Christian service has been right in your home, with aging relatives or growing youngsters.

Perhaps your task has been one of social or political action as you have been gripped by the need to proclaim God's justice to those with secular power. Or maybe you have stood your ground on behalf of those who are too socially marginalized to speak for themselves. Perhaps your mission has been to work for those of our neighbors whom we never know in person but whose voices reach us from the places of oppression elsewhere in the world, or whose voices have been silenced by hunger, imprisonment, or death. And in all of this, you have looked to God for guidance, have done the best you could, and in turn have been given grace for the task at hand.

Then why do I need to join a Covenant Discipleship Group?

The first reason has already been given: You are being called by Christ to take a new step in your discipleship. But there is another reason, and it has to do with your maturity as a Christian disciple. The more we follow Christ the more we grow in grace. As with all growth, this takes place when we are not aware of it, then something happens to let us know that we have changed.

Such experiences are common in the natural life. We can all remember as a child finding that we could reach a shelf that used to be too high. Many of us discover in middle age that our clothes have "shrunk," though we cannot recall exactly when. We remember what it was like to have someone confide in us for the first time, letting us know that we had grown to be trustworthy. Perhaps we can recall being taken seriously in a conversation by an older person, with our own point of view respected for the first time. We never quite know when and how these changes take place, but from time to time we become aware that we have grown in new ways and that we are moving forward in life.

We grow in grace in ways we do not comprehend. Indeed, the more we grow in grace the more we discover our need of growth. The more we walk with Christ the more we realize how much we lack the strength merely to keep pace. Our growth as Christian disciples is essentially a matter of learning how to hold fast and how to stay the course. This is why it takes time to become mature in our discipleship.

At first we tend to devote ourselves to Christ with all of our own energies, and often these are quite considerable. But gradually we find that the only way to sustain our relationship with Christ and to follow his teachings is to rely more and more on the grace of the Holy Spirit. This is the path to Christian maturity. This is how we "grow in Christ."

Then, from time to time and almost always unexpectedly, we reach a stage in our pilgrimage where our need of grace becomes particularly clear to us. There is a point in our discipleship at which we become acutely aware of our inability to be spiritually self-sufficient. And with this awareness comes a new and profound understanding of how much we need help.

This is also true if we have been actively involved over the years in Christian service to the world. We have probably been aware for a long time that we cannot change the world overnight. But we may not have perceived until now that the only way we can be effective for the coming reign of God is to be ready for the particular tasks Christ assigns to us. Once again, the key is obedience, not just service. And in this too we need the help of trusted Christian friends and colleagues who will support us and hold us accountable.

If these answers touch on why you have felt the need to join a Covenant Discipleship Group, then you have come to a new maturity in your Christian discipleship.

How will joining a Covenant Discipleship Group affect my Christian friends or family who do not wish to join?

If you are asking this question, you are probably concerned that joining a Covenant Discipleship Group may make other people in the church perceive you as a "superChristian," or as someone who is going to make everyone else feel awkward or inferior. You are right to be concerned, because spiritual elitism, the feeling that some of us have the "inside track" with God, is not a desirable quality.

You can quickly be assured that belonging to a Covenant Discipleship Group will not make you a spiritual elitist, nor will others perceive you as such. In fact, Covenant Discipleship Groups have a role in congregational

There is a point in our discipleship at which we become acutely aware of our inability to be spiritually self-sufficient.

life and work that is as discreet as it is effective. A good illustration is the church choir, which likewise has a special role to play in the life and work of the church. It would be easy for the congregation to regard the choir members as superior. After all, as they process through the sanctuary, finely robed, to prominent seats in the chancel; they seem to be highly privileged. Yet there are two reasons why they are not regarded as superior church members. First, they are doing a job on behalf of the rest of us: they are helping us worship. And second, they give up one night a week to practice. They have a talent, but they must apply themselves to use it; and when they do, it is for the benefit of the whole congregation. Moreover, if we had the time and the inclination, we could join them; for very seldom is anyone excluded from a church choir because of the quality of his or her voice.

"That's all very well," you may reply, "but Covenant Discipleship involves more than music and worship. In a Covenant Discipleship Group I am going to be accountable for what I do in all the dimensions of my Christian discipleship: my good works, my spiritual disciplines, my very understanding of God's will in my life. Surely that is going to single me out in the congregation as someone who makes other people feel inadequate."

You can be assured that this too will not happen. As you give your time and energies to a disciplined walk with Christ, people will look on you and your Covenant Discipleship Group as a contribution to the mission and ministry of the congregation as a whole. They will realize that your role is to help give all of them a better understanding of their own walk with Christ. They will begin to look to you for guidance and advice. You will become a leader in discipleship.

Moreover, as you hold yourself accountable week by week, you will come to know better than anyone that you have no grounds for feeling superior. You will come to understand more clearly why the Christians at Ephesus were told that only in Christ could they boast.

What will happen to me in a Covenant Discipleship Group?

The short answer is that you can expect to become more consistent, more reliable, more dependable in your Christian discipleship. But there is more to it than that. You can expect three things to happen: You will become more aware of God's grace in your life. You will find new ways of serving God and your neighbor. You will find your understanding of God's will greatly enhanced.

You will become more aware of God's grace in your life. Because God's grace is extended to us with gracious hospitality, we must exercise our gracious freedom to allow grace to work in and through us. This means taking a realistic view of our sinful tendency to resist God's gracious initiatives. It means taking responsibility for allowing God to work in our lives, and for obeying the teachings of Christ in our discipleship.

As you engage in mutual accountability week by week, you can expect to become more regular in your attendance at worship, in receiving the sacrament of Holy Communion, in your prayer life, and in your Bible study. Perhaps you will begin the spiritual discipline of fasting or temperance, and through your Covenant Discipleship Group you will begin to experience the

For by grace you have been saved through faith, and this is not your own doing; it is the gift of God—not the result of works, so that no one may boast. For we are what he has made us, created in Christ Jesus for good works, which God prepared beforehand to be our way of life.

(Ephesians 2:8-10)

richness of true Christian conversation (Christian conferencing).

These means of grace will give you new strength and vigor for your Christian life. You will not experience this all at once, nor will it happen predictably. You will continue to have many times of routine worship and devotion, and your new times of blessing will catch you by surprise. But most assuredly, as you open yourself more consistently to the means of grace, the Holy Spirit will empower your discipleship.

Then, from time to time God will let you know that you are becoming a seasoned Christian disciple. It may be through a new insight into the Scriptures, or in a quiet but dramatic answer to prayer, but these moments will become more intimate and more holy than you ever thought possible.

The faithfulness of a dependable Christian disciple is always honored by the God who not only loves us with parental love but also thrives on the love that we give. As returned prodigals, we should never forget that God desperately wants the whole family back home.

You will find new ways of serving God and your neighbor. For many group members this proves to be the most exciting aspect of Covenant Discipleship. When you begin your weekly meetings, you will probably find yourself where most of us were before joining a Covenant Discipleship Group: a faithful church member, bearing no one in particular any ill will, and helping people in ways that make for good neighborly relations. You have probably been quite intentional in these good Christian habits.

In your Covenant Discipleship Group, however, you will discover opportunities for acts of compassion you have never considered before. At first this may seem disconcerting, especially when you realize just how much the horizons of your neighborliness need to be stretched. But week by week you will find yourself impelled by grace to serve newfound neighbors. Perhaps you will find them in prisons, among the homeless of your community, or among disadvantaged children struggling to survive the drug culture.

You will acquire a bolder and clearer vision of the coming reign of God, the new age promised by Jesus Christ. This will give you new opportunities to further God's justice in the world. Perhaps you will be prompted to take a stand on issues such as the death penalty, political torture, racism, or world hunger. You may find yourself standing against less dramatic issues at your place of work that nevertheless require an active witness to God's justice. You may even find yourself making such a stand in your church, where injustice can as readily be found. These involvements will be all the more unnerving if they are new for you, but always God's grace will be sufficient for the tasks that Jesus assigns.

Likewise, if you have been involved in these issues for many years, your Covenant Discipleship Group will bring new perspectives to your acts of compassion and justice. As you encourage others to reach out to those in need, in turn you will be touched by the need for small kindnesses close to home. You will find yourself drawing more consistently on the means of grace and thus find your discipleship more truly obedient to Jesus Christ. It is all too easy to forget in whose service we expend our time and energies.

You will find your understanding of God's will greatly enhanced. When Jesus instructed the first disciples to meet together in his name with the promise that he would always be in their midst, he was not offering them a spiritual bonus. He was stating a truth of Christian discipleship: We need one another in order to discern the will of God.

The reasoning is quite straightforward. When you and I are in communication with God, one end of the line consists of a very imperfect receiver. Whatever God is trying to say to you or me, our own agendas are likely to get in the way, and we do not hear or even listen clearly. But when several of us gather together, each endeavoring to listen to God, and each committed to helping the others with their discipleship, the insight and the discernment of the group gives each one of us a better idea of what God is trying to do with our lives. As each person gives an account of how he or she has tried to walk with Christ, together you will arrive at a level of responsiveness to grace that none of you would have acquired on your own.

When you join a Covenant Discipleship Group, you must expect the grace of God to invade your life in new ways. The presence of Christ in your midst is not a promise of convenience and comfort. The grace that flows through channels being kept open by the weekly accountability will come in ways that are both inconvenient and uncomfortable and that you are often not quite ready for.

As we have noted, the General Rule of Discipleship will shape your life more intentionally around acts of compassion, devotion, worship, and justice. You will experience the love and power of God in new ways. Your prayer life will be more effective, your worship more inspiring, your service to others more fulfilling, and your work for God's justice more compelling. The promptings and warnings you receive from the Holy Spirit will be unnervingly direct, and you will have new hope for the ultimate fulfillment of the reign of God, the kingdom of God, on earth as in heaven.

Being mutually accountable for our discipleship is not a self-improvement exercise. Rather, in a Covenant Discipleship Group we open ourselves to the gracious initiatives of the Holy Spirit as promised to us by God in Christ Jesus. In opening us to the will of God, Covenant Discipleship proves to be a powerful means of grace.

Conclusion

In addition to what has already been offered, I will add two more first steps: Read this handbook and subscribe to *Covenant Discipleship Quarterly*.

This handbook is not only a guide to Covenant Discipleship but is also a collection of comments and advice to help the group understand its role in relation to the mission and ministry of the congregation as a whole. The handbook will also impart a sense of the tradition of Christian small groups that has shaped Covenant Discipleship.

Covenant Discipleship Quarterly provides continuing resources for Covenant Discipleship Groups. In addition to the nuts and bolts of Covenant Discipleship, *Covenant Discipleship Quarterly* includes samples of group covenants, suggestions for more effective group meetings, notice of special events and workshops, and much more. See page 79 for information on how to receive *Covenant Discipleship Quarterly*.

As part of a Covenant Discipleship Group, you will experience the love and power of God in new ways. Your prayer life will be more effective, your worship more inspiring, your service to others more fulfilling, and your work for God's justice more compelling. The promptings and warnings you receive from the Holy Spirit will be unnervingly direct, and you will have new hope for the ultimate fulfillment of the reign of God, the kingdom of God, on earth as in heaven.

Part 3

Forming and Sustaining a Covenant Discipleship Group

Restore to me the joy of your salvation,
and sustain in me a willing spirit.
(Psalm 51:12)

Writing and Implementing the Covenant

Once a Covenant Discipleship Group has been formed and the members have agreed on a day and time to meet, the first task is to draw up a covenant of discipleship that will be the basis for weekly meetings. As you write your covenant, you will find it helpful to follow the balanced approach of the General Rule of Discipleship. This will focus the covenant on all the teachings of Jesus rather than on the strengths or preferences of your members. Existing groups have found three components to be essential for most, if not all, covenants: a preamble, individual clauses, and a conclusion.

On pages 68–75 you will find sample covenants as well as samples of preambles, clauses, and conclusions used by Covenant Discipleship Groups. Several points about these sample clauses are worth noting. First of all, while they are arranged according to the categories of the General Rule of Discipleship, not all of them can be clearly defined as acts of worship, justice, devotion, or compassion. Indeed, in some instances there is considerable overlap and even duplication.

These overlaps and duplications illustrate an important principle of the General Rule, and of the whole of Christian discipleship: We should not get caught up in method for its own sake. It is far more important to have clauses that are meaningful and relevant to the Christian life than to have clauses that are neatly classified. When we walk with Christ, we are on a journey with a real person; and while the teachings of Jesus give us important guidelines, our discipleship will always be relational and, therefore, full of surprises.

Another point worth noting is that a number of clauses illustrate ways in which the ongoing accountability of Covenant Discipleship Groups deepens the insight and conviction of its members. This is reflected in clauses that become more specific and challenging either in the frequency with which a particular intention is put into practice or by the directness with which the clause identifies particular disciplines or tasks. Some of the examples indicate this development. This is not an expression of overachievement but merely an indication that grace is at work in the lives of the members as they begin to chew on the solid food of the gospel.

I fed you with milk, not solid food, for you were not ready for solid food.

(1 Corinthians 3:2a)

One final word, these examples are included in the hope that they can assist you in writing your covenant. They are certainly not meant as rigid rules for your discipleship or that of your group. Together you must develop your own covenant, with Christ and Christ alone as the model for your discipleship, and the Holy Spirit as your guide.

The Preamble

The preamble states the nature and purpose of the covenant, making clear that it is not a set of rigid regulations but rather a shaping of Christian discipleship in response to God's grace. The writing of the preamble often raises significant points of faith and practice, so it is important to encourage members to express opinions freely as the preamble is developed.

You may write your own preamble or use one of the samples in this book. If you use one of the sample preambles, feel free to change the wording or to substitute something altogether different. If you choose to write your own preamble, the process may take several weeks; but it is important to avoid getting caught up in discussions around minor details. If need be, go on to writing the clauses and come back to the preamble later. One of the most devious snares for a Christian is to talk about discipleship rather than practice it!

The Clauses

Although there is no hard and fast rule, covenants typically contain eight to ten individual clauses. These clauses reflect the teachings of Jesus as summarized in the General Rule of Discipleship, as well as the balance between acts of mercy and acts of piety. The most important thing to be said about the clauses is that since each group writes its own covenant, the covenant must contain only those clauses that every member is willing to accept as a guiding principle of his or her discipleship.

Having said that, there are exceptions to that rule. While individual clauses must be agreed upon by all members of the group, it is possible for covenants to include "personal clauses" for members who may wish to be held accountable for a particular aspect of discipleship that clearly does not affect the others. Groups respond to this need by agreeing to leave time at the end of each weekly meeting to hold the particular member accountable for these personal clauses. These do not have to be written down but can be shared with the rest of the group week by week, especially since they will tend to be of immediate and temporary concern.

As with the preamble, there are often lengthy discussions before clauses are agreed upon. Take as long as necessary, since these clauses are statements of intent and will be the touchstone of the group's journey in discipleship. They must be something that each member can wholeheartedly affirm in faith and practice.

The Conclusion

When the preamble and the clauses have been completed, a short statement reaffirming the nature and purpose of the covenant will bring it to a conclusion and will express the intent of the group to shape their lives according to the covenant and to be held accountable for keeping it. Whatever is written, the conclusion must emphasize that grace is the dynamic of discipleship. Members are not striving to maintain standards or levels of performance but are instead seeking to follow the teachings of Jesus in their lives, trusting that the Holy Spirit will empower them in their walk with Christ.

Once all aspects of the covenant are agreed upon, a member of the group should accept responsibility for having it reproduced so that everyone will have a copy. All members should then sign their own personal copy and bring it to each weekly meeting, where it will be the blueprint for mutual accountability. Some groups reduce their covenant to a small laminated card, making it even more convenient to carry around.

Additional Suggestions for Writing the Covenant

In order for Christians to be in communion with God, they must not withdraw from the world; so make the clauses relevant. Clauses must reflect the worldly context of the group and acknowledge that God's grace reaches us right where we are in the world. In order to be responsive to God's grace in the routines of daily living, feel free to introduce clauses for a limited time or to drop clauses that are no longer relevant. The discipline of discipleship is learning how not to resist the gracious initiatives of the Holy Spirit.

Make the clauses of your covenant practicable without compromising accountability.

Make the clauses of your covenant practicable without compromising accountability. Although this may mean initially reducing the requirements of a particular clause, avoid those that are too demanding for any member. The question to be asked is whether a clause is doable, whether it is something that everyone feels can be attempted with a reasonable expectation of accomplishment.

Take as an example the clause in the sample covenant concerning the Eucharist: "I will receive the sacrament of Holy Communion each week." If there are group members who object to this, the wording can be changed to "each month." If there are still objections, the wording can be changed to "regularly." Since Holy Communion is an instituted means of grace, however, the clause should not be dropped altogether.

As another example, some members may object to a clause that states, "I will spend four hours each month to help the disadvantaged." The wording may be changed to something more general, such as, "I will be sensitive to people in need and help them when I can," though again, as one of Jesus' commandments and as a component of the General Rule, the clause should not be dropped altogether.

Once the regular discipline of weekly accountability begins to become routine, be prepared to change clauses occasionally in order to make them more challenging. This will happen in several ways as the covenant helps the group to mature in its discipleship. For example, the group may discover that a clause that has received only token attention suddenly acquires new meaning. At these moments of growth the group will want to consider "taking up the slack" by making the relevant clauses of the covenant more challenging.

A good example is the clause from the sample covenant (page 75) that states, "I will heed the warnings of the Holy Spirit not to sin against God and my neighbor." After weeks of routine answers, someone may ask, "Who is my neighbor?" The answer Jesus gave to that question is always a challenge (Luke 10:25-37). Or the group may be confronted with the question of what it means to receive a warning of the Holy Spirit. The group may find itself in critical consciousness raising as the meaning of inward discernment is revealed with new depth and power.

Or perhaps the group deals with the clause on prayer in a somewhat routine manner until one of the members reports that her child has asked her during the past week why their family does not say grace at mealtimes. Out of this discussion comes a general confession from the group that no one is holding family prayers and that something should be done about it.

The initial covenant is not cast in stone but is a flexible, dynamic, and resilient framework for a discipleship that will always be responsive to the grace of God. As with all healthy guidelines, covenants are designed to maintain the balance of our walk with Christ. They are not ends in themselves but are the means to an end. The only inflexible aspect of the covenant is our commitment to become more dependable and reliable in our discipleship.

In the sharing of spiritual insights, joys and concerns, strengths and weaknesses, the burdens of the world, and the hope of God's saving righteousness, Christian disciples find the grace of God more and more sustaining as they watch over one another in love and learn to lose themselves more profoundly in the will of God.

Some Common Questions

Because the covenant is so central to the life and work of Covenant Discipleship Groups, many questions are asked about its nature and purpose. Following are examples of questions most frequently raised, along with some possible answers.

Why do we need a covenant?

We need a covenant because a covenant relationship with God is the foundation of Christian discipleship. We make our covenant in response to the gracious initiative of the Holy Spirit, and God promises to accept us as family, with all of the privileges that brings. Our part is to accept our new family obligations, joyfully serving God in every way we can.

If our covenant is with God, why do we need to make a covenant with one another?

This question is more difficult to answer today than in earlier generations. Today agreements tend to be taken seriously only when they prove convenient, and this attitude has infected the church. Most covenants made by Christians today, whether with God or with one another, are of very short duration. We plan their obsolescence, preparing at the outset for the time when we may no longer want to keep them. In short, the word *covenant* has become seriously devalued, and as a result a great deal of discipleship has become optional.

By contrast, if we take our discipleship seriously and regard the keeping of our word as a point of honor, then a covenant with one another makes very good sense. There are at least two things of which we can be assured in our covenant relationship with God: (1) God will always be faithful; (2) many times we will not. Accordingly, those of us who are concerned about being good disciples should at least seek to minimize our faithlessness and do all we can to avoid breaking our covenant with God.

This is what makes the covenant with one another so important. As with most things in life, the best way to insure that we do something faithfully is to do it with others of like mind and purpose. A covenant with other Christians provides us with the mutual support and accountability we need in order to keep our covenant with God.

Does the covenant tend to become legalistic?

Not when we remember that we enter into it mutually and willingly. Moreover, since each group writes its own covenant, the clauses have the consensus of the group right from the beginning. If a covenant seems to be legalistic, the group needs to revise it and recover ownership of it.

Does a written covenant inhibit the freedom of grace?

Not at all. Without an agreed statement of intent such as the covenant, it is all too easy for Christians to shape their discipleship around their own preferences and even prejudices. This has rightly been labeled cheap grace, a grace always readily adaptable to personal convenience.

The freedom of grace in Christian discipleship is not the freedom to live our lives as we wish but rather the freedom to avoid the enslavement of our own desires and ambitions. Perhaps the most important discovery of Christian disciples is to realize how ill equipped we are to run our own lives. The covenant of discipleship helps us hold fast to the freedom of God's will rather than our own, to surrender an illusory freedom for the true freedom of binding ourselves to Christ.

Why does this have to take the form of a written covenant?

There are certain basic guidelines for discipleship given to us in the teachings of Jesus. As was noted earlier, Wesley summarized these as works of mercy and works of piety, which are incorporated into the General Rule of Discipleship as acts of compassion, acts of devotion, acts of justice, and acts of worship. However much we advance in the Christian life, we never outgrow the need for these basics. While the Holy Spirit may increasingly empower us in our discipleship, the structure of a written covenant provides the form of how we live it out in the world. It is a framework within which we deepen our relationship with Christ while holding fast to the priorities of our obligations to Christ.

Once it is written, can the covenant be changed?

Covenants need to be changed regularly in order to maintain relevance. There are two kinds of changes. Occasionally groups will relax clauses that have proven to be too demanding. But more often than not they will tighten clauses rather than loosen them. As grace shapes their discipleship, members wish to be held more, rather than less, accountable.

The Group Meeting

Once a covenant has been written and signed, the group is ready to begin the regular format of weekly meetings. The only hard and fast rule for these sessions is that they must last only one hour. Meetings are to begin on time, whether or not everyone has arrived. And they are to end promptly, even if they began a little late. If members wish to continue meeting beyond the hour, it is best to end the session and then move into an informal time of sharing for those who wish to stay.

While some groups feel that this approach is too strict, it is best to keep in mind that Covenant Discipleship Groups are not designed for fellowship, even though a great deal of fellowship occurs. Covenant Discipleship

Groups are designed for mutual accountability. They are business meetings in which the business is Christian discipleship.

Every member needs to know from the outset that one hour is the only time that will be required of them. This way they are free to plan other activities before or after the meetings and to schedule the group meetings in the midst of busy schedules—at any time of the day, on any day of the week. Most members are grateful for the firm limit of one hour. People who need to get to work after an early morning meeting, or back to work after a noon meeting, can count on a prompt conclusion. They know that a Covenant Discipleship Group can readily be scheduled in conjunction with other activities. The agenda is such that extensive preparation for the meeting is unnecessary. One merely has to come prepared to be honest with one's Christian colleagues, and with God.

Various Covenant Discipleship Groups meet at 6:00 A.M. on Monday mornings, 10:00 P.M. on Sunday nights, and many times in between. The noon hour is popular for those who can get away at lunchtime. Some groups meet in the late afternoon between leaving work and returning home, while others meet at 6.30 P.M. on Wednesdays just before the time that many churches have midweek activities scheduled. Since Covenant Discipleship should not substitute for a Sunday school class, few groups meet on Sunday mornings, although a very popular time is late afternoon or early evening on Sundays.

The group must also agree on a regular meeting place. Although it is okay for groups to meet at a different place each week, there is a drawback. Members must remember the different arrangements, and moving around can lead to uncertainty about the location. Established groups have found it best to find a regular place that is relatively convenient for everyone.

While there is no problem with meeting in homes or places of work, most groups opt to meet at their church. Care should be taken in selecting the room. Where possible, avoid large rooms as well as those where interruptions are likely to occur. Although the format of a Covenant Discipleship meeting is quite structured, there is still a degree of intimacy. Members must be completely at ease during the entire hour in order to feel free to express themselves in an atmosphere of confidentiality.

If a regular meeting place is not possible, or if members prefer to take turns in offering hospitality for the group, then the meeting place for the next meeting must be clearly stated at the conclusion of each meeting, and care must be taken to ensure that absent members are told as soon as possible. One of the worst things a group can do to itself is have people guessing each week about where they are going to meet.

Leading the Group

Each Covenant Discipleship session must have a leader, although this is not a permanent role. Leadership of the group rotates, with each member taking a turn. If any member is hesitant about accepting leadership responsibilities, do not press the point. Although everyone is encouraged to assume this role in due course, leading the meeting is not a condition of belonging to the group.

Covenant Discipleship Groups are designed for mutual accountability. They are business meetings in which the business is Christian discipleship.

To avoid unnecessary tension, it is often helpful to have a leader appointed for the first few weeks. If a member has had experience in group dynamics, that person is the logical choice. If the pastor is a member of the group, he or she can assume the role. Once the form of the meetings has become familiar, however, the leadership should rotate.

The distinctive format and dynamic of Covenant Discipleship is found in the dialogue between leader and members. The early church called this format catechesis, a process of questions and answers that enabled the early Christian community to teach its children as well as its new members. The catechist was the questioner, and the learners were called catechumens. In a number of denominations even today, learning one's catechism remains the first step toward being accepted into full church membership.

Although the content of the catechesis in Covenant Discipleship Groups is practical rather than doctrinal, the method is the same. Important aspects of Christian discipleship are, first of all, agreed upon and written into the covenant. The leader for the week reads and responds to each clause and asks each member to do likewise. In this way, the guidelines for living a Christian life are written, heard, and spoken.

Through the covenant, a basic checklist is agreed upon, a routine is established, and members work through each clause, one by one. The procedure is elementary but necessary. After all, serving Jesus Christ in the world is the most important responsibility we have. It deserves to be taken seriously.

Group meetings must always be opened with a short prayer, either by the leader for the week or by another member. This prayer is primarily a request for the guidance of the Holy Spirit and for an openness on the part of members to whatever God's grace may seek to accomplish and whatever avenues are needed: assurance, sympathetic understanding, firmness, and even correction when necessary. It is important that everyone be ready to receive God's word, and this attitude of readiness can be accomplished at the outset of the meeting with a well-worded prayer.

Many groups find it helpful to have the entire covenant read aloud, either by the leader or by the group as a whole, although some may find this to be a little reminiscent of elementary school and may resent the implications. It is important to remember that the wording of the covenant has been laboriously honed, and in many instances the covenant is an eloquent document. Since it is the bedrock of the group, the covenant deserves an oral reading.

After the opening prayer and the reading of the covenant, each clause of the covenant is taken in turn as a point of accountability. Beginning with herself or himself, the leader asks each member whether the intent expressed in the clause has been fulfilled during the past week. The questions are asked without any implied judgment but rather as a means of sharing a joint pilgrimage and of "watching over one another in love."

If the member responds that the clause was fulfilled, the leader asks if the member had any noteworthy happenings or experiences that might help other group members in their journey. If the member responds that the clause was not fulfilled, the leader asks if the member encountered any special difficulties and whether the group can be of any help to the member in observing the clause more faithfully. Only when each member has answered does the leader proceed to the next clause.

This dynamic of catechesis differs from other types of group discussion and reinforces the importance of the leader in maintaining the flow. Although it is helpful to select a leader for the first few weeks who has some appreciation of group dynamics, it is also important to have the leadership rotate as soon as possible. If the role of leader is permanently assigned to one person, that person does not really have the opportunity to share in the process of mutual accountability.

The leader must always keep an eye on the time so that the meeting flows toward the end of the hour and not past it. The leader must also encourage all members to participate and keep overly talkative members in check. In other words, leading the group is hard work; if that load is not shared by everyone, one member of the group (the leader) is going to be at a permanent disadvantage.

As far as possible, the entire covenant should be covered each week. However, as relationships develop and as people begin to talk about their discipleship more openly, it may not be possible to go through all of the clauses in the time available. The leader should therefore exercise discretion as to which clauses will be covered during the meeting, and group members should be held accountable the following week for any clauses that have to be omitted.

In the interest of time, the leader may combine several clauses into one round of catechesis. For example, prayer and Bible study may be taken together. Particular clauses concerning acts of compassion may be combined, as may clauses concerning acts of justice. Worship and sacrament go well together, and clauses related to temperance or fasting may be linked with clauses on spiritual promptings.

Combining clauses is often necessary during the early meetings of the group. By the same token, if members are having difficulty with a particular clause, they may wish to spend some time discussing or revising it and limit the time for answering the other clauses. However, it is important to remember that no aspect of the covenant should be regularly postponed or combined. If this starts to happen, the group should reconsider its covenant and perhaps make some revisions. Clauses that are not a vital part of the group's accountability are detrimental to the covenant as a whole and should be dealt with.

The leader should always keep in mind that the purpose of the group is to be accountable to the covenant. This should not make the conduct of the meeting unduly rigid, but neither should the conversation be allowed to digress into matters of general or casual interest. This is where the format of catechesis, or question and answer, proves to be helpful in keeping the meeting on course. The occasional exchange between members should certainly be allowed as a spontaneous dimension of the meeting, but the leader should resume the role of catechist as soon as possible.

The skill to be acquired in this catechesis is primarily that of controlled dialogue, known in small-group terminology as feedback. At times a group member will need to be encouraged to reply with more than a yes or no. At other times a member may need to be discouraged from dominating the conversation with lengthy accounts of personal experiences.

The extent to which this is handled tactfully but firmly will depend largely on the feedback given by the leader in response to each of the members. It is the leader who must move through the covenant at an appropriate pace and determine whether an extended exchange with a member can be of value to everyone else. It is also the leader who must, as Wesley put it, "advise, reprove, comfort, or exhort" the members, offering guidance, correction, affirmation, or encouragement (From "Journal From September 2, 1770, to September 12, 1773"). These skills are not acquired right away, but they come much more readily than in many small groups, in part because of the rotation of leadership but also because of the commitment of the group to a mutual accountability. The more each person practices leadership skills when it is his or her turn, the more honest the group becomes in its accountability, and the more effective members become in their discipleship.

At times the group will experience deep Christian community. This is bound to increase as the group members develop relationships with one another. Although this deep sense of communion is to be welcomed, it should not become the objective of the meeting. The purpose of each session remains accountability for the covenant, and the tone of the weekly meetings is polite rather than intense. Although this may be an initial disappointment for members who are searching for meaningful experiences of community, it is ultimately a source of profound reassurance. More intimate communion becomes a spiritual bonus, not a weekly expectation that quickly becomes a burden.

A meeting that is formal, even mechanical, is just as important for the integrity of the group as one that is rich in spiritual sharing. In the long run, such a meeting is even more important. Numerous studies have demonstrated that people behave differently in small groups and tend to be more open with their feelings. In the hands of a skilled professional, this vulnerability can be used to great therapeutic effect, and often is. But when guided by unskilled leaders, people in small groups often say things they do not mean to say and react in ways they subsequently find embarrassing or even humiliating. The formal catechesis of Covenant Discipleship and the agenda of an agreed covenant of intent are important safeguards against such a pitfall. Weekly meetings are much more concerned with what people have done than with what they feel, and this prevents delving into areas that group members are not equipped to handle. It also means that the group can function effectively without professional leadership.

Yet, even with the safeguard of catechesis, personal problems may emerge during group meetings from time to time, and members must not feel inhibited about raising them. Nor should other members regard them as an intrusion, since they may provide an opportunity to help the affected member as well as other members with the same problem.

Once again, however, the leader should not allow personal problems to

Weekly meetings are much more concerned with what people have done than with what they feel.

distract the group from the covenant. A helpful solution can be to introduce the next clause but at the same time offer to stay at the end of the meeting to talk further, asking other group members who can to stay afterward as well. This allows the person who raised the problem to consider how much he or she really wants to talk about it, and may provide an opportunity for all involved to assess whether it is something that really ought to be referred to the pastor.

Just as the Covenant Discipleship meeting opened with a prayer, it should also be closed with prayer. This can take a number of forms, from a brief benediction, to individual concerns, to a more focused time of intercession. Some groups ask the pastor of the church to join them during the closing minutes and celebrate a brief service of Holy Communion. This is most manageable when several groups are meeting at the same time and in the same location. Having gone through their respective covenants, several groups can come together in one room for closing worship.

Groups with an ordained clergy person as a member may close with Communion whenever they wish. But for groups without a clergy member, pastors are usually more than willing to celebrate the Eucharist, one of the highest privileges of ordained ministry.

Various other housekeeping items should be attended to before the meeting concludes. If there are any personal clauses for which individual members have asked the group to hold them accountable, these should be covered. Likewise, any personal clauses for the next week should be noted. All members of the group will want to share responsibility for contacting those who are absent. Although absences are generally due to unforeseen circumstances, it is always good to be held accountable in order to maintain the integrity of the covenant. In addition, if the absent member proves to need help in some way, the group can respond quickly or notify the pastor.

An important housekeeping item is to choose a leader for the next week. Once the group is well established in its routines, serving as leader requires no major preparation. But during the first few months, and especially for those who have not done this sort of thing before, it is helpful to have a week's notice. It is always a good thing for the leader to prepare for the meeting prayerfully.

Before leaving, the members must always be clear about any particular aspects of their discipleship on which they need to act, whether it be in compassion, justice, worship, or devotion, or in obeying the promptings and warnings of the Holy Spirit. A final declaration of intent at the end of the weekly meeting can be helpful.

Introducing Covenant Discipleship Into the Congregation

Just as muscle does not make up the whole body, so it should not be expected that every member of a congregation will wish to make a commitment to a Covenant Discipleship Group. Even though a covenant of discipleship includes nothing that a person does not promise to be and to do when joining the church, the extent to which this commitment is lived out, or even understood, will depend on where the person is in his or her pilgrimage with Christ.

If it seems surprising that not everyone would choose to be in a Covenant Discipleship Group, given that the disciplines of such groups are really quite minimal, it must be remembered that people respond to God's grace in different ways, with varying degrees of commitment, and with varying degrees of faith. Seeds are planted, but God does the harvesting in God's own time. The essential dynamic of Christian discipleship is our response to grace; and while Christ remains constant, disciples of Christ manifest a wide range of response.

This diversity of responses has been confirmed by the many congregations that have begun Covenant Discipleship Groups. When the recommended procedures have been followed, approximately fifteen percent of the membership who are regularly at worship are ready to take part in a Covenant Discipleship Group. This does not mean, however, that the opportunity to join a Covenant Discipleship Group should not be given to all church members, and given repeatedly. Church members will wish to make a deeper commitment to their faith at certain points in their pilgrimage and should feel free to do so in the environment of their local congregation.

Covenant Discipleship Groups have proven to be an excellent way of keeping such vocational steps constantly available, providing not only the opportunity to commit to Christian discipleship but also the encouragement to further that commitment. However, before describing the process of introducing Covenant Discipleship Groups into the congregation, I will offer two extremely important cautionary words. The first cautionary word relates to the role of the pastor, the second concerns the nature and length of the commitment being made by the members.

Pastors are pivotal to the success or failure of Covenant Discipleship Groups; however, they may need to be convinced of their value and validity before the groups can contribute anything to the ministry and mission of a congregation. This statement is not meant to imply that Covenant Discipleship Groups require intensive pastoral supervision. They do not. One of the strengths of Covenant Discipleship is the speed with which groups become self-supervising and self-supporting. But before they can be integral to the life and work of the church, the pastor must be certain of their function in relation to everything else that takes place in the congregation.

If the pastor is not convinced of the validity of Covenant Discipleship Groups, there is little likelihood that the groups will ever become an effective part of a congregation. Through preaching, through pastoral care, through countless private conversations and public exchanges in which a

The essential dynamic of Christian discipleship is our response to grace; and while Christ remains constant, disciples of Christ manifest a wide range of response.

pastor shares, the concept of Covenant Discipleship can be affirmed or denied. This is why it is vitally important that the pastor be a member of the first group to be formed.

The second cautionary word concerns the nature and length of commitment to Covenant Discipleship. If there is a distinguishing characteristic of Covenant Discipleship, this is it. To join a Covenant Discipleship Group is not to exercise a preference but to respond to a call. Group members need to understand this at the outset so that they in turn can affirm it for the rest of the congregation. Those who join a Covenant Discipleship Group must understand that their commitment is open-ended; that is, it is most likely to be for the remainder of their Christian life.

Of course, an open-ended commitment to Covenant Discipleship does not imply lifetime membership in the same group. This will rarely be possible, given the nature of our mobile society. People change jobs and homes; schedules frequently change. But in joining a Covenant Discipleship Group, Christians make a commitment to be accountable for their discipleship. By definition, this means a permanent change in lifestyle and priorities.

When this is made clear at the outset, some people will hesitate and in some instances will decide that this is not a commitment they wish to make at this point in their Christian pilgrimage. Most people considering Covenant Discipleship, however, find it to be an affirming word that locks them into their decision and their calling. The attrition rate from Covenant Discipleship is quite minimal.

Introducing Covenant Discipleship Groups

The most effective way of introducing Covenant Discipleship Groups to a congregation is through pilot groups. These meet for at least a year, testing the format and preparing the congregation for the time when the groups are opened to the whole congregation. Pilot groups allow a congregation to consider carefully what impact Covenant Discipleship will have on its life and work. The word *pilot* is not used to mean experimental. Members of pilot groups are not "trying out" Covenant Discipleship to see if it is worthwhile any more than Jesus invited his disciples to follow him for a trial period. Pilot groups take the lead in exploring Covenant Discipleship Groups on behalf of the congregation. They find out about Covenant Discipleship Groups by actually forming one.

Pilot groups use the same guidelines that are used by established groups and establish many of the procedures that will integrate groups into the congregation. There are several practical advantages to starting Covenant Discipleship with pilot groups:

• Pilot groups provide a source of leadership and expertise when the groups are introduced on a wider basis.

• During the pilot year, groups raise people's awareness of the concept of Covenant Discipleship and spread the word throughout the congregation. Questions and objections can be raised and answered so that the membership at large can look forward expectantly to the forming of more groups.

• Pilot groups place no undue administrative burden on the pastor or the church staff. Between the formation of a pilot group and the opening of groups to the rest of the congregation there is ample time to prepare for the logistics of wider participation.

• Pilot groups are able to explore Covenant Discipleship on behalf of the congregation without the pressure of success or failure.

The number of pilot groups depends on the size of the congregation. In most instances, one pilot group will suffice. But in larger congregations, and especially where there are multiple staff members, two or even three pilot groups may prove feasible. Experience has shown, however, that there should be no more than three pilot groups; otherwise they tend to assume more than a pilot role and become the sort of administrative burden they are designed to avoid.

As already noted, it is important that the pastoral staff of the congregation take part in the pilot groups. In congregations where there will be only one pilot group, a pastor should be a member. In larger churches, other staff may be assigned to second and third pilot groups. Although staff members may serve as leaders during the first few weeks by contributing some basic skills in group dynamics, the purpose of having them in each group is not to provide permanent leadership. Rather, staff participation says clearly that Covenant Discipleship is integral to the life and work of the church, a place where the basics of discipleship are practiced and where discipleship is modeled for the congregation.

Contrary to some pastors' fears, taking part in a Covenant Discipleship Group does not compromise their pastoral role. Meetings focus on how the members are living out their Christian discipleship in the world. The content of each meeting is quite objective, focusing much more on what people have done than on what they have experienced. In the doing of discipleship, the basics are the same for all Christians, clergy or lay; and pastors need to be accountable for these basics no less than anyone else.

Interestingly, once pastors do take part in such a process of accountability, they and the other group members find a new understanding of one another. It becomes clear that the most natural support group for a pastor is not other pastors but the pastor's own parishioners. In the relatively short space of one hour, and with the clear agenda of an agreed covenant, there is little risk of entering into the deeper sort of sharing that might encroach on issues of pastoral confidence. However, there is ample opportunity to sense the common journey that pastor and people share together. This mutual discovery almost always becomes an occasion of deepened understanding.

One of the most heartening aspects of implementing Covenant Discipleship Groups is to find out just how many church members have been waiting for something like this to be offered. Most congregations have members willing to make themselves accountable for their discipleship. The recruitment of pilot group members can thus be very matter-of-fact: announcements from the pulpit, in the worship bulletin, and so forth.

In most instances, such announcements will produce enough responses to form at least one pilot group. If this does not happen, then a more intentional invitation must be made. The pastor can make a direct approach to those members of the congregation who have shown their willingness over the years to engage in active Christian witness and service. An approach can likewise be made to those members who are searching for a deeper understanding of their faith.

Another way of extending a more intentional invitation is to arrange for presentations to various groups in the congregation such as Sunday school classes or continuing education events. The Accountable Discipleship Office of the General Board of Discipleship (see page 79) may be able to recommend someone from a roster of trained consultants who will come to your church for a training event.

Whichever method is used, the fact remains that most congregations will have at least a few members ready for the sort of commitment offered by Covenant Discipleship. When these people are informed about it and sense that the pastor is willing to make it a full component of the ministry and mission of the church, they will respond.

Occasionally a congregation may find that there are too many volunteers for the maximum of three pilot groups. If this happens, it is strongly recommended that a fourth pilot group not be formed, for the reasons already given. A request can be made for volunteers to withdraw from the pilot process and to wait until the following year when the groups will be opened to the entire congregation.

By the same token, while a pilot group can remain open to new members during the first month of its meetings, it should be closed for the remainder of the pilot year. Changes in membership tend to be disruptive for groups involved in something new, and they should be allowed the freedom to concentrate on their task. If people with an especially high level of interest are unable to join a pilot group during its first month, their interest can be sustained by involving them in preparations for the weekend when the groups are opened to the entire congregation (see page 52).

In all other respects, pilot groups function just like every other Covenant Discipleship Group. As pilot groups, they are doing what other groups will do in a year's time. Pilot group members should feel free to exercise a degree of flexibility in their meetings, since they are the first in the congregation to be exploring the guidelines and procedures outlined in this book. However, they must at no time lose sight of their role as pilot groups. Others in the congregation will be ready in a year or so to benefit from their expertise as they form additional groups. When that time comes, the experience and the testimony of the pilot group members will be of vital importance.

An important dimension of the pilot process is letting the other church members know that Covenant Discipleship is being explored with a view to incorporating it into the total ministry and mission of the congregation. This means that members of the pilot groups should make every effort to talk to others about what is happening in their meetings. Confidentiality should be protected, but there is much that can be shared in a

An important dimension of the pilot process is letting the other church members know that Covenant Discipleship is being explored with a view to incorporating it into the total ministry and mission of the congregation.

number of ways with the membership as a whole. Settings might include

• Sunday school classes: Members of pilot groups can offer to make a presentation in which they describe Covenant Discipleship Groups and answer questions people may have.

• Sunday morning worship: A brief word of testimony from a pilot group member can be very effective during the time allocated for announcements and the sharing of congregational concerns.

• Church organizations: Opportunities abound for sharing information with the Administrative Board or Council, United Methodist Women, United Methodist Men, United Methodist Youth Fellowship, and others.

The recommended span for the pilot process in Covenant Discipleship is one year, though this is not a rigid recommendation. Sometimes the pastor and the group will sense a readiness among the members that requires the date to be brought forward. In most instances, however, a year will be needed for pilot groups to do their work thoroughly. This allows them to experience the growing sense of grace that binds a Covenant Discipleship Group together in its obedience to Jesus Christ. It also allows them to experience and grow through some of the difficulties encountered in the discipline of accountability. To use a "muscle" of the church that has not been activated for some time will probably mean some aches and pains until it is in shape, and it usually takes a year for this to happen.

Most important of all, a year's experience enables the members of pilot groups to provide sure guidance to the new groups when they are formed. Covenant Discipleship cannot be effective if it is planted in shallow ground. It must be planted deep for a rich harvest of discipleship; and as any gardener knows, seed planted deep always takes longer to germinate.

Pilot groups must begin with the clear objective of opening Covenant Discipleship to the whole congregation approximately one year later. This will take the form of a special Covenant Discipleship weekend, described below. A date for this weekend should be placed on the church calendar, with publicity arranged well in advance.

The extension of covenant groups to the whole membership is a critical transition for the congregation. A number of members will form new Covenant Discipleship Groups, taking a step forward in their own discipleship. But it will also be the birthing of a new understanding of discipleship throughout the congregation; and, as with all births, there will be a degree of unpredictability about it. The pilot group members should therefore be watchful as well as ready in preparing for this culmination of their work.

The Covenant Discipleship Weekend

A Covenant Discipleship weekend is a proven way of opening Covenant Discipleship Groups to the congregation as a whole. As already noted, not everyone will be ready to join a group; but it is vitally important that everyone be invited to join. In this way the entire congregation can feel a sense of ownership and have a stake in this new dimension to their ministry and mission. In addition, those who make the commitment

Not everyone will be ready to join a group, but it is vitally important that everyone be invited to join.

to join a group can be affirmed in their decision without the rest of the membership feeling that Covenant Discipleship is in any way exclusive.

Scheduling the Weekend

Many congregations have found early spring or early fall to be a good time to schedule a Covenant Discipleship weekend. The only sure guideline for determining the date is the point at which pilot members feel they have come to understand the nature and purpose of Covenant Discipleship and can confidently share it with everyone else in the congregation.

Inviting a Guest Leader or Preacher

The advantages of having an outside leader and preacher for the weekend are the same as for any special event: fresh insights and perspectives, affirmation of Covenant Discipleship from an independent source, and freedom for the pastor and pilot group members to provide support as full participants.

Leading a Covenant Discipleship weekend requires a sensitive understanding of the groups as well as the ability to preach a direct invitational sermon. The Accountable Discipleship Office (page 79) may be able to recommend a trained person who can help lead the event. However, there is usually no one better qualified to preach and lead the weekend than the pastor of the congregation and pilot group members. Having worked together in Covenant Discipleship for at least a year, they will be sensitive to the level of readiness for this new commitment within the congregation. Therefore, while a guest leader and preacher can often enhance a weekend, there are few instances in which such a person is absolutely necessary.

Preparing the Pilot Group Members

I have already stressed how important the pilot group members are for the introduction of Covenant Discipleship. Their participation in this weekend is no less significant. Their testimony to what has been happening during the pilot year is one of the most effective aspects of the event, and their role in helping new groups get started is indispensable. Well in advance, therefore, the pilot group members should be prepared for the part they will play in the weekend.

First, they should be ready to give an account of their pilot group experience. There are formal occasions during the weekend when they will be called upon to do this, but there will be a number of informal occasions as well. This is not to say that their testimonies should be overly prepared, since spontaneity will be their most effective quality. However, it may be a good idea to have a practice session ahead of time. Many people are hesitant to give personal testimonies, and a "dry run" can often help them overcome apprehension. Members must be encouraged to be quite candid in what they say. As pilot members, they have been leading the way for the congregation, and they must not conceal the difficulties of Covenant Discipleship any more than they will wish to downplay the advantages.

Helping Start New Groups

When asked for their help to start new groups, pilot group members often ask whether they have to disband their existing groups and divide themselves among the new ones. This question has an interesting track record in Covenant Discipleship, and there is no short answer.

When the pilot process was first introduced, a strong recommendation was that the pilot members divide up among the new groups following the congregational introduction weekend. This recommendation quickly encountered resistance from members of pilot groups who did not want to leave their original group. As a result of this understandable resistance, a compromise procedure was suggested. If a pilot group did not wish to disband after the Covenant Discipleship weekend, members were asked instead to give an hour each week to provide leadership for a new group during its formative stages while continuing to meet with their own groups. Once the new groups had found their feet, pilot members could withdraw and revert to meeting only with their own group, which by then had become one of a number of Covenant Discipleship Groups in the congregation.

In the intervening years, reports have been received from congregations on the effectiveness of both procedures. Without exception, when pilot groups disbanded and divided themselves among new groups, the results were much more positive than when they agreed to merely "do overtime" for a few weeks. Groups who adopted the compromise suggestion reported that they wished they had resisted the appeal of staying together.

The answer to the question of whether or not pilot groups should disband is therefore a qualified affirmative. Yes, they should disband except where there is such stiff resistance that it would prove detrimental to the groups as a whole.

Publicity and Materials

The weekend should be well publicized in the life and work of the congregation. The event should be intentionally promoted as a critical turning point in the life of the congregation. To regard the weekend as merely another programmatic offering would be self-defeating. It is nothing less than the launching of a whole new generation of leaders in discipleship and must, therefore, be given appropriate emphasis.

As a final preparation for the Covenant Discipleship weekend, order and have on hand other Covenant Discipleship resources. Suggested resources and instructions for ordering are listed on page 79. For the most current information on Covenant Discipleship, check the General Board of Discipleship Web site at www.gbod.org. The weekend will generate a high level of interest in Covenant Discipleship, and the resources will be useful for those who join groups as well as for the congregation as a whole.

The Format for the Weekend

The following paragraphs describe a format for a Covenant Discipleship weekend that has been effective in a wide range of congregations. It should be stressed, however, that Covenant Discipleship Groups are designed to develop leadership in congregations; and insofar as each con-

The Covenant Discipleship weekend, which introduces Covenant Discipleship Groups to the whole congregation, should be intentionally promoted as a critical turning point in the life of the congregation.

gregation has distinctive characteristics and traditions, the format may be considered adaptable to different contexts.

The purpose of the weekend is to extend the invitation to all of the congregation to join a Covenant Discipleship Group. Therefore, whatever is most effective in reaching the membership as a whole must govern the shape and the planning of the event.

Friday: The weekend should begin on Friday evening. It is helpful to begin with a churchwide meeting such as a covered dish supper or a family evening with dessert or refreshments. Afterward, the pastor or the guest speaker should give an introduction to the concept of Covenant Discipleship, followed by the pilot group members talking about their experiences of the past year. Their testimonies are invariably a high moment in the weekend.

This is a good time to air and discuss any lingering doubts or objections. The speaker and pilot group members form a panel to answer questions in a time of dialogue. As the discussion unfolds, all the ways in which the pilot group members have been breaking the new ground of Covenant Discipleship on behalf of the congregation will quickly become apparent. It is reassuring for everyone to hear that joining a group is a response to God's call and not something that is expected of everyone in the church.

If there is a guest speaker for the weekend, he or she will need to meet the pilot members beforehand and agree how to divide the available time during the evening. It is best if the presentations and panel discussion can be kept to about one hour. The objective is simple: to leave the audience with a clear picture of what a Covenant Discipleship Group is and what is involved in joining one.

Saturday: On Saturday, preferably in the morning, a two-session training seminar should be held. The first session should present an account of the theology behind Covenant Discipleship Groups and something of their origin in the Methodist tradition. The second session should include a practical explanation of how a Covenant Discipleship Group functions, with members of pilot groups inviting other participants in the seminar to join them in performing a short roleplay of a typical weekly meeting.

The value of this roleplay cannot be overemphasized. It does not have to go through the whole of a covenant, but it should include a sample clause from each of the four areas of the General Rule of Discipleship: compassion, justice, worship, and devotion. It should also include the other procedures of a weekly group meeting described in this handbook: an opening prayer and reading of the covenant, concluding prayer concerns, agreement on who will be the leader for the next week, personal clauses, and any actions the group has agreed to take with regard to the covenant. Afterward, the seminar participants, in dialogue with the roleplayers, reflect on what has happened, a discussion that often raises the most meaningful questions of the entire morning.

The roleplay shows more convincingly than anything else that Covenant Discipleship Groups are not at all threatening but are, rather, an assurance of comradeship on a common journey. It also provides a clear demonstration of mutual accountability in forging a faithful discipleship.

Since seminar participants are invited to join the pilot group members in playing these roles, there is no opportunity to rehearse. As a result there is almost always a spontaneous outpouring of relief and delight as the roleplay proceeds. This sense of relief reveals a mutual concern for everyone's discipleship, and a mutual need to be in company with those of like mind and spirit. In addition, even though this is in a training context, roleplays reveal that the Christian journey is not solitary exercise and that there are trustworthy companions along the way.

The purpose of the Saturday seminar is to provide a more detailed introduction to Covenant Discipleship than is possible on Friday evening. At the same time, it allows the pilot members to interact with people who are likely to become the nucleus of the congregation's new Covenant Discipleship Groups. A warm collegiality must be extended by the pastor and the pilot group members to the seminar participants. One way of doing this is to explain that during the worship service on Sunday an invitation will be extended to those who wish to participate in a Covenant Discipleship Group. Ask the participants to be thinking about whether or not they want to be a part of a group, and encourage them to plan to come forward as the invitation is given on Sunday. It helps considerably to have a good initial response to this invitation; and if those who intend to join a new group will come forward promptly with the pilot group members to make their commitment, others will be encouraged to follow.

When there is a guest speaker for the weekend, it is helpful to schedule a Saturday evening meeting with the administrative leadership of the congregation. The purpose of this session is not to recruit them for group membership but to ask for their support in accepting Covenant Discipleship as a new dimension of the ministry and mission of the congregation. The integration of these groups into the life and work of the church is vital to the groups' purpose and effectiveness, and such a meeting can greatly facilitate that integration process.

If there is no guest speaker, this support can be sought at regular administrative meetings prior to the weekend. Even so, such a meeting can still be helpful to make sure that there are no misunderstandings about Covenant Discipleship or its place in the leadership of the congregation.

Sunday: The high point of the weekend comes during Sunday morning worship service, when the invitation to join a Covenant Discipleship Group is made to the entire congregation. The order of worship should indicate clearly that the focus of the service is to call people to embark on a journey of mutual accountability for their discipleship. The hymns should center on service and obedience to the will of God, and the text for the sermon should reflect the theme of working out our salvation. Possible Scriptures include Matthew 21:28-32 and Philippians 2:12-13.

A clear indication must be given that following the sermon an invitation will be extended for members to make a public commitment to becoming accountable disciples through participation in a Covenant Discipleship Group. This can be done by including in the bulletin a sample covenant of discipleship such as the one on page 75.

The invitation to join a Covenant Discipleship Group is the most important moment of the weekend, and it should be extended without

The Christian journey is not solitary exercise, and there are trustworthy companions along the way.

any pressure or manipulation. Those who are ready will make their commitment in response to the Holy Spirit. All they need is a simple, straightforward invitation. At the same time, it should be made clear that those who respond are making their commitment as part of the church's ministry and mission. They are being asked to come forward as a public act of dedication so that the congregation as a whole can affirm them in their decision and support them in their weekly disciplines.

The liturgy, the music, the Scripture readings, and the prayers can all assist in preparing for this moment. But there must also be a place in the order of service for a brief description of Covenant Discipleship, including what is involved in joining a group and how the weekly meetings are conducted. At this point the sample covenant in the bulletin insert can be used to demonstrate that there is nothing unusual about a covenant of discipleship. The only difference is that members of a Covenant Discipleship Group agree to be accountable for keeping it.

At the conclusion of the sermon, an invitation to join a Covenant Discipleship Group should be extended. Those who wish to respond should be asked to come forward and stand at the front of the sanctuary while the organist plays quietly. It is best not to have a heavy silence at this point, nor is it a good idea to have people respond during the singing of a hymn. People need time to make their decision prayerfully, and it may take several minutes for everyone to come forward from different places in the sanctuary.

The background music should continue until all movement has ceased, at which time the guest preacher or the pastor should lead those who have come forward in a prayer of commitment. "A Covenant Prayer in the Wesleyan Tradition" (*The United Methodist Hymnal*, 607) is a good choice.

Conclusion and Open Invitation

Following the prayer, the worship leader should thank the people for making their commitment and inform them of a short meeting to be held following the service at which new Covenant Discipleship Groups will be formed. If there are any who cannot attend, they are asked to sign the sample covenant in their bulletin and leave it with an usher or at the church office so that they can be contacted during the following week. The worship leader should also announce to the congregation that those people who felt unable to make their formal commitment in the service are still welcome to come to the meeting after the worship service. Furthermore, the Covenant Discipleship Groups are now open for everyone to join at any time. There are no conditions for joining other than a willingness to commit to the weekly meeting and an intention to follow the clauses of the group covenant.

All people should then be asked to return to their seats, and the worship service should continue. This symbolic reuniting of the people with the congregation further ensures that the whole body affirms the decision of these members to join Covenant Discipleship Groups, and that the groups are a fully recognized dimension of the congregation's ministry and mission.

I am no longer my own, but thine.
Put me to what thou wilt, rank me with whom thou wilt.
Put me to doing, put me to suffering.
Let me be employed by thee or laid aside for thee,
exalted for thee or brought low by thee.
Let me be full, let me be empty.
Let me have all things, let me have nothing.
I freely and heartily yield all things to thy pleasure and disposal.
And now, O glorious and blessed God, Father, Son, and Holy Spirit,
thou art mine, and I am thine. So be it.
And the covenant which I have made on earth,
let it be ratified in heaven. Amen.

("A Covenant Prayer in the Wesleyan Tradition")

Sustaining Covenant Discipleship Groups in the Congregation

One of the major advantages of Covenant Discipleship Groups for the local congregation is that relatively little direct supervision is required. With an agenda centered on the General Rule of Discipleship's acts of compassion, justice, worship, and devotion, and focused on how members are living as Christians in the world, weekly meetings provide a structure within which group members can reliably hold one another accountable for their discipleship and can respond in the power of the Holy Spirit.

However, even with this advantage Covenant Discipleship Groups do not just happen. Like any other small group in the congregation, they need to be cared for and nurtured. If ignored, they will gradually cease to function.

On the one hand, the very format of a Covenant Discipleship Group, with its routine and repetitive series of questions and answers, makes such a group extremely susceptible to boredom and dryness, and emptiness and loss of interest on the part of some or all of the members. If nothing is done to help a group through such times, it may well lose its sense of purpose.

On the other hand, the agenda of Covenant Discipleship Groups raises expectations and widens the horizons of group members. There is a high level of commitment when members begin their weekly accountability and embark on this journey with Christ that opens new opportunities for discipleship. If these opportunities are not provided through the ministry of the congregation, Covenant Discipleship Groups can easily become self-centered and introspective, more concerned with their heightened expectations than with living out their discipleship. This in turn leads to frustration with the weekly process of accountability as meetings become simply a litany of what they know they ought to do but are not doing.

These various housekeeping issues have led to the realization that Covenant Discipleship Groups themselves must be watched over in love no less than their individual members. This realization has led to the creation of several new leadership roles and opportunities within the congregation. The following ideas for nurturing Covenant Discipleship Groups through the use of conveners, coordinators, quarterly meetings, and covenant meals have proven to be effective in a number of different congregational settings.

Unlike the group leadership, which rotates each week, the position of Covenant Discipleship convener is a continuous appointment and is filled when the Covenant Discipleship Group is first formed, usually following a Covenant Discipleship weekend.

Conveners are people within Covenant Discipleship Groups through whom the pastor or the church office can maintain regular contact. The responsibilities are not heavy, but conveners are a significant liaison, providing ready access and serving as a link between pastors and groups. In congregations with a number of Covenant Discipleship Groups, regular meetings between the conveners and the pastor provide an arena in which the progress of the various groups can be monitored. Suggestions can be made for providing groups with opportunities to exercise their discipleship in new ways, and resources and problems can be shared. It is by no means uncommon for a group to gain new momentum by learning what another group has done in similar circumstances.

As with anything in the life and work of the church, if Covenant Discipleship Groups are neglected or taken for granted, they will not thrive. And since Covenant Discipleship is a long-term commitment, all groups require careful and constant oversight. Conveners meet that requirement.

Once Covenant Discipleship Groups become well established, it is a good idea to appoint a layperson to act as the coordinator, or contact person, within the congregation. The coordinator can provide administrative support for all of the groups, preside at meetings of conveners, and act as liaison with the pastoral staff. When a coordinator is appointed, the position should be confirmed by the charge conference in the same way that other leadership of the church is confirmed. It should be incorporated into the administrative structure of the congregation as a means of linking it with the wider ministry and mission of the church.

In addition to regular meetings for the conveners, it is helpful to hold meetings from time to time for all group members; and in some congregations this has become a quarterly event. This quarterly meeting can take various forms but is primarily an opportunity to provide additional resources for the groups. Guest speakers can be invited not only to address particular areas of discipleship in depth but also to direct members to further opportunities for service. The General Rule of Discipleship can serve as guidelines for these meetings so that acts of compassion, justice, worship, and devotion receive due attention in turn.

Another way to nurture Covenant Discipleship Groups is the covenant meal. Held in conjunction with a quarterly meeting or on its own, the covenant meal has emerged in recent years as a significant means of grace in congregational life. The meal is sacrificial, with very simple food, and is followed by a time of sharing around the table, during which group members tell stories of discipleship out of their own experience or that of other Christian disciples. The atmosphere is similar to the early Methodist lovefeast, as the stories affirm the boundless nature of God's grace. And on those occasions when Christians from other countries are present, the testimonies are all the more powerful and eloquent.

The covenant meal is also a time for the sharing of pain and suffering, most especially the hurts of the world beyond the congregation, that might otherwise remain comfortably hidden and obscure. It is quite appropriate to receive an offering where members contribute what they would otherwise have paid for a full meal, and to use the money for the work of the church among the poor and the hungry.

Another important function of the covenant meal is that it provides the opportunity to invite prospective group members to experience Covenant Discipleship in a very direct way. For those who have shown interest but have not yet made the decision to join a group, meetings such as this are an open and non-threatening introduction to the nature and purpose of

If Covenant Discipleship Groups are neglected or taken for granted, they will not thrive.

Covenant Discipleship. It invites others to see the interaction of the members, hear the stories of discipleship coming out of the groups, experience the presence of the risen Christ as faithful disciples gather around a meal table in his name, and be blessed by the inviting grace of the Holy Spirit.

Recruitment of New Members

The covenant meal is not the only means of recruiting new members for Covenant Discipleship. Indeed, once the groups are functioning in a congregation, regular invitations should be extended by group members and pastoral staff. This can be done in any number of settings: from the pulpit, in Sunday school classes, at midweek meetings, and in all of the informal contacts of congregational life and work.

There are two conditions for receiving new members into a group. The first condition is that new members understand the nature of the commitment and are willing to accept the covenant presently in use by the group. There are regular opportunities for changing the covenant, but welcoming a new member is not one of them. This condition is not meant to deny new members full participation in the group, or to place them on any kind of "probation." Instead, it is meant simply to introduce new members to the mutual accountability of Covenant Discipleship. Opportunities to share in subsequent revisions of the covenant will come later.

The second condition for accepting new members is that they will be invited to attend the group for three meetings before making the decision to join. During these visits, they should be given the option of taking part in the process of accountability or merely observing. Prospective members will be limited to three visits before being asked to make their decision. The reason for the limitation is the format of the weekly meetings. Unlimited participation by those who are undecided will quickly prove disruptive, whereas limited visits of this nature can readily be assimilated.

As we have noted, the only time a Covenant Discipleship Group is closed is during the pilot year. Thereafter, new members may join at any time and are encouraged to do so. It is fundamental to the role of the groups in a congregation that they be perceived not as secretive or mysterious but as an open and continual opportunity for making a contribution to the life and work of the church of Jesus Christ. It stands to reason that if those who first joined the groups had reached a point in their walk with Christ where they needed to take another step forward in their commitment, others are going to reach the same point and will be ready to respond to the same invitation when it is regularly extended.

An excellent opportunity for inviting people to join a Covenant Discipleship Group is Covenant Sunday, a Methodist tradition that has been neglected in recent years but is now being revived in a number of congregations. The tradition goes back to John Wesley and the annual Covenant Service he instituted for early Methodist societies. An order of worship for the Covenant Renewal Service can be found on page 288 of *The United Methodist Book of Worship*. The service has been revised several times since Wesley's time, but it remains a powerful and eloquent statement of Christian covenant with God.

Once the groups are functioning, regular invitations should be extended for members of the congregation to join a group.

For many years Methodists made this Covenant Service a watch night service on December 31. They would gather for worship in the closing hour of the old year so that the first act of the new year could be the renewing of their covenant with God. Later traditions observed it on one of the Sundays after the Epiphany. Whichever tradition is observed, Covenant Sunday provides an opportunity for some creative worship, especially in a congregation where Covenant Discipleship Groups are established.

Existing groups can review and publicly renew their covenant. Individual members can be asked to give a short presentation to the congregation, testifying to what this disciplined commitment has meant for them and for the mission of the church. And the invitation for others to join Covenant Discipleship Groups once again affirms the reality that they are integral to the life and work of the whole congregation.

Covenant Sunday is also a good time for groups to review their meeting schedules and change the day and time if need be. It may also be an opportune time for individual members to change groups if needed for scheduling purposes. Some congregations intentionally disband all of their groups prior to Covenant Sunday, thereby allowing members to stay together, change groups if they wish, or form totally new groups.

In summary, Covenant Sunday can be an annual acknowledgment of Covenant Discipleship Groups for what they are: a means of grace for the church. Those who join a group are making themselves accountable for their walk with Jesus Christ so that through their methodical discipleship the whole congregation might better serve the world in ministry and mission. This commitment needs to be affirmed as often as possible, and Covenant Sunday provides just such an opportunity.

Covenant Discipleship Beyond the Congregation

As Covenant Discipleship has spread throughout the United States and to a number of other countries around the world, it has proven to be adaptable for use in contexts other than the local congregation. The natural habitat of the groups remains the congregation, where they help develop leaders in discipleship. But this need not limit their setting to congregations. The practice of mutual accountability can also be exercised in settings where people come together for other purposes, or where weekly meetings would not be feasible.

The most common adaptation of Covenant Discipleship is for clergy support groups. In many parts of the country, and especially where collegiality is difficult to sustain because of distance, such groups have begun to use Covenant Discipleship as a component of their meetings. It should be noted that Covenant Discipleship is not suitable as the sole format of a clergy group. When it is the only planned agenda, Covenant Discipleship tends to be subsumed by other forms of sharing and discussion. When Covenant Discipleship is a component of clergy support groups, however, it can often be the key to everything else that happens. A time of mutual accountability centered on the General Rule of Discipleship can set a tone for the meeting that enhances other discussion and sharing. This is especially the case when the time of Covenant Discipleship makes up the first part of the meeting. The intentionality of this opening hour almost always directs the group into richer sharing and exchange.

Care must be taken, however, not to allow clergy support groups to take the place of congregational Covenant Discipleship Groups, for it is in the local congregation that Covenant Discipleship Groups are ultimately most productive. While members of clergy support groups can benefit from Covenant Discipleship within these support groups and can learn a great deal about its nature and purpose, they should implement groups in their congregations as soon as possible.

Such a move will have two positive effects. First, it will direct pastors toward their primary support group: members of their congregations. By nature, clergy are "congregational animals." This is their calling, and this is where they find fulfillment. Second, when clergy belong to a Covenant Discipleship Group in a congregation as well as to a clergy support group, it frees the clergy group for deeper professional and personal interaction. Dialogue can be more open, and mutual accountability more particular. If clergy support groups engage in this sort of collegial exercise without being accountable for the basics of Christian living, their discussions become abstract and their agenda progressively introspective. But when the members are holding themselves accountable for these basics through Covenant Discipleship Groups in their congregations, their support groups can move into areas of discipleship that are uniquely the concern of clergy. Clergy covenants of discipleship can then focus on the pastoring of their congregations in ministries of compassion, justice, worship, and devotion. Their mutual accountability can open up aspects of their work that need to be shared with trusted colleagues. And clergy have the sure knowledge that because of the weekly accountability in their congregational groups, they are not avoiding the basics of their discipleship but building on them.

A clergy support group that incorporates Covenant Discipleship as part of its meeting might draw from the following suggestions, each of which is designed as a one-hour segment for a monthly meeting. The group can draw on as many of these as it wishes, or as many as it has time for.

• Use of a covenant written and agreed upon by the group, in which the clauses may be more particular than those of a typical Covenant Discipleship Group, though they should cover all dimensions of the General Rule of Discipleship; The role of leader for this hour should rotate, as in other Covenant Discipleship Groups, and mutual accountability should be exercised just as faithfully.

• A report from members of the group on the progress of Covenant Discipleship Groups in their congregations, including personal reflections on how the groups are affecting the discipleship of the clergyperson in particular and of the congregation as a whole;

• A discussion of some agreed passage of Scripture, or a volume of devotional or prophetic literature;

• A time of intercessory prayer, with a diary kept by the group to note concerns and needs;

• A concluding worship service including the sacrament of Holy Communion.

As personal sharing grows out of any of these activities, it should be allowed to develop spontaneously. But there should always be a planned agenda, and leadership responsibilities should be assigned on a rotating basis, not only for the Covenant Discipleship part of the meeting but for all segments.

These suggestions for clergy support groups can just as readily be incorporated into other contexts. People who meet on committees, task forces, commissions, and boards, find that an hour of their time devoted to Covenant Discipleship can greatly enrich their meetings. In some annual conferences, the cabinet and the conference council staff incorporate Covenant Discipleship into their meetings, holding themselves accountable for their work on behalf of the church. Where meetings are relatively infrequent, as in the case of a national board or committee, some members have agreed to hold themselves accountable by mail, e-mail, or telephone between their times together. Whatever the context, however, the principles remain the same: Keep the one hour Covenant Discipleship format distinct, either preceding or following the other agenda of the meeting. Use a shortened covenant suitable for the context of the meeting but still shaped by the parts of the General Rule of Discipleship: compassion, justice, worship, and devotion.

Though all of these possibilities are important, the most important contribution of Covenant Discipleship Groups is the extent to which they help train leaders in discipleship for local congregations. Individual members are, of course, helped personally by the weekly meetings. But the true purpose and function of the groups is to exemplify methodical, reliable discipleship. By holding themselves accountable for witnessing to Christ and for living out his teachings in the world, Covenant Discipleship Groups can help form faithful Christian disciples and empower congregations to be more vital in ministry and mission.

If Covenant Discipleship Group members are to provide this leadership, they must be allowed to assume their proper role in the life and work of congregations. Their insights will be unexpected, sometimes critical, but almost always a source of spiritual discernment on boards and committees; in Sunday school classes; in youth groups; and in the church's ministries of compassion, justice, worship, and devotion. They will not necessarily occupy traditional positions of leadership, but their influence will be substantial—*if* they are acknowledged as leaders in discipleship, and *if* their groups are carefully formed and nurtured.

To recognize the leadership of Covenant Discipleship Group members is really a matter of common sense. They are the members of a congregation who are practicing the discernment of God's will and who are methodically practicing obedience. Their accountability week by week gives them a heightened sense of Christ's vision of peace and wholeness and a deeper awareness of the promptings of the Holy Spirit that draw us and nudge us toward the reign of God. These disciples need to be heard and heeded as their leadership develops.

Much of this sort of leadership will be implicit in the various ways that Covenant Discipleship Groups participate in the life and work of the

By holding themselves accountable for witnessing to Christ and for living out his teachings in the world, Covenant Discipleship Groups can help form faithful Christian disciples and empower congregations to be more vital in ministry and mission.

congregation. Certain group members, however, are going to develop leadership qualities that are more explicit. Their spiritual discernment will be more sensitive, their knowledge of human beings more astute, their organizational abilities more evident, and their pastoral concern more focused. These members will do more than practice mutual accountability in the tradition of the early Methodist class meeting. They will also be potential pastoral leaders who, working with the staff of the church, can transform a congregation from a flock that constantly demands feeding to a company of disciples who will assist with the work of Jesus Christ: feeding the little ones of the world. Congregations that recognize such people for who they are will also want to commission them for what they can do.

There are Christians today, no less than in Wesley's day, who are ready to accept such a call, ready to fulfill their discipleship through a method of mutual accountability. But there are also those whose pilgrimage in the Christian faith has not yet brought them to this point, who come to church primarily to be fed, and healed, and taught, and loved. The challenge that faces us, therefore, is how to be accepting of both the few and the many in the life and work of the congregation; how to nurture a large, inclusive church while at the same time acknowledging the accountable disciples for who they really are: mentors in the faith.

Simply put, the most important lesson we can learn from the early Methodist class meeting is in the area of congregational leadership. If we accept that an accountable disciple is a role model for the Christian life, then congregational leadership takes on a whole new shape. Instead of being entrusted to professional staff with appropriate "programmatic skills," leadership becomes a dynamic fusion of the particular gifts and graces of accountable disciples, both clergy and lay.

The distinction that then emerges is not between skilled and unskilled leaders but between those who are ready to be held accountable for their discipleship and those who are not. The question is not so much discerning who has gifts and graces but who is prepared to use them. It is not a matter of training but of commitment. The watchword is not exhortation but example.

The prevailing view of pastoral leadership in the church has blurred this distinction, with the result that many clergy are overburdened with tasks they were never meant to handle, and many laypeople who are ready to assume leadership roles are denied the opportunity. But once the leadership of congregations is defined in terms of accountability for discipleship, it becomes clear that we must draw the distinction afresh.

It is precisely this sort of leadership that Covenant Discipleship Groups are designed to foster. Covenant Discipleship Groups do not preclude other faith-forming groups in the life and work of the church. On the contrary, they often strengthen them with enhanced leadership and participation. But they do have a very particular function. They focus on a mutual accountability for the basics of Christian living in the world. Shaped by the General Rule of Discipleship, they draw together the "methodical" disciples of today.

Covenant Discipleship Groups do not preclude other faith-forming groups in the life and work of the church. On the contrary, they often strengthen them with enhanced leadership and participation.

As Wesley made clear to us more than two hundred years ago, Christian discipleship is rarely experienced as spiritual growth, even though growth does take place and is to be expected. Faithful discipleship, lived out in the power of the Holy Spirit according to the guidelines of Jesus Christ, is much more a matter of holding fast, doing the best we can with the gifts we have received and in the freedom and responsibility of joyful obedience. Covenant Discipleship Groups are for those who wish to share in that commitment so that the church as a whole can more effectively serve Jesus of Nazareth, the one who has been named to preside over the coming reign of God.

Two Warnings and a Promise

The commitment made by members of Covenant Discipleship Groups almost always causes an infectious exuberance, and in the first few weeks of the meetings there are many positive experiences. The hunger for this sort of firm accountability is real, and it will also be accompanied by the fascination for something new and exciting, from which none of us is altogether immune. Therefore, as new groups are formed and begin to meet, it is important to issue two warnings to them.

The first warning concerns the "doldrums." The practice of being accountable for aspects of discipleship that have previously been neglected or taken for granted gives each group a wealth of insight and challenge during the first few months of meeting together. After three or four months, however, a sense of routine sets in. The questions seem to become mechanical, answers lack spontaneity, and members begin to question the validity and usefulness of the whole exercise.

It should be clearly stated to new groups that this time of doldrums is to be expected for two reasons. The most immediate cause is the wish to turn to something new when the novelty of the groups has worn off. In part, this is reflective of our culture's preoccupation with self-fulfillment, and it should be resisted. Indeed, withdrawing from religious "junk food" is one of the most important functions of Covenant Discipleship Groups.

However, there is also a deeper, spiritual reason for the doldrums that can best be described as "getting a second wind." Most churchgoers today are out of practice when it comes to accountable discipleship. Many have allowed themselves to become spectators in church, watching and perhaps admiring those who seem to be committed to their faith, though not really wishing to join them in the work of Jesus Christ. Now that they are in a Covenant Discipleship Group, however, there is no avoiding the challenge of discipleship. While this is at first exhilarating, there comes a time when the routine of the task begins to take hold and when the daily grind requires stamina.

As a group gets this second wind, it should be explained that this is exactly what Covenant Discipleship is all about. It is an agreement to watch over one another. We are in covenant not merely to share the high points of our journey, important though these are, but much more to sustain and support one another in the midst of the routine and commonplace.

The second warning regards the danger of complacency about accountability. When this happens, it usually takes the form of thoughtless, or worse, dishonest answers. These are infectious, putting the group at a serious disadvantage and having an adverse effect on the meetings. Groups should know in advance that this is a real danger to their purpose and well-being.

Suggestions have been made in preceding sections about ways the leader can address such problems each week. But a general word of advice based on reports received from many groups is that if complacency is a problem in a group, time and again the reason proves to be procrastination. The members have reached a point where the grace of God is impelling them to take another step in their discipleship, but they are putting it off, holding out against grace. Put simply, members of the group are being disobedient, the very thing Wesley warned would shipwreck a Christian's discipleship.

A group suffering from complacency, therefore, should ask itself a candid question: What are we not doing that we have been clearly prompted to do by the Holy Spirit? The answer will probably be simple, obvious, and doable. So do it!

And now for that promise. If a group remains faithful to its covenant through the doldrums and complacency, it is not long before the rough and tumble of living in the world brings the members to realize even more profoundly the value of their common bond. Such times of apparent aimlessness are no more than a test of the commitment the members have made, a searching and tempering of their discipleship, a moving away from interests that are self-serving to those that are Christ-serving. It is a form of spiritual growth well attested to in the history of the Christian faith, but groups need to know about it at the outset and be ready for it. John Wesley's words still ring loud and clear, calling us to accountable discipleship:

> We go on from grace to grace, while we are careful to "abstain from all appearance of evil," and are "zealous of good works," as we have opportunity, doing good to all men; while we walk in all His ordinances blameless, therein worshiping Him in spirit and in truth; while we take up our cross, and deny ourselves every pleasure that does not lead us to God.
> (From Sermon 43, "The Scripture Way of Salvation")

Part 4

Additional Helps

Your hands have made and fashioned me;
give me understanding that I may
learn your commandments.
(Psalm 119:73)

Examples of Covenant Preambles

Having been called by Jesus Christ to be disciples, with awe and trembling hearts we answer his call to be doorkeepers. This group will exist for the purpose of support, communal prayer, receiving the Word, and watching over one another in love so that all are encouraged to work out their salvation and offer others Christ.

Christian disciples need a firm foundation of faith. Paul urges the church at Ephesus to "grow up in every way . . . into Christ" so that they may no longer be children "tossed to and fro and blown about by every wind of doctrine" (Ephesians 4:13-15). To that end, that we may grow toward maturity of faith and celebrate as a community God's presence with us and the gifts God has given us to use for the furthering of the Kingdom, we expect of all who join us . . .

Called into being and empowered by the grace of God, we covenant to dedicate ourselves to a life that exemplifies Christ and the gospel. We offer our time, talents, abilities, and resources in obedience to the gospel, acknowledging our dependence upon God's grace and the power of the Holy Spirit.

As Christians we acknowledge God's unconditional love and acceptance of all creation. God is alive in us and guides us on our journey of faith. With these things in mind, we will support and encourage one another in our efforts to follow God's plan for our lives. We will strive to recognize God as strength, salvation, love, peace, inspirer, comforter, friend, hope, joy. In order to more fully develop our relationship with God, we covenant to do the following: . . .

I love you, O LORD, my strength.
The LORD is my rock, my fortress, and my
    deliverer,
      my God, my rock in whom I take refuge,
      my shield, and the horn of my salvation, my
      stronghold.
I call upon the LORD, who is worthy to be praised.
                    (Psalm 18:1-3a)

In gratitude for the grace of Jesus Christ, in whose death and resurrection we have found new life, we pledge to be his disciples. We recognize that our time and talents are gifts from God, and we will use them to search out God's will for us and to obey. We will do our best not to compromise the will of God for human goals. We will serve both God and God's creation earnestly and lovingly. We respect and accept fully all group members, whose integrity and confidentiality we will uphold in all that we share. With God's grace and their help we covenant to . . .

Knowing that Jesus Christ died for me and that God calls me to be a disciple of Jesus Christ, I desire to practice the following disciplines in order that I might know God's love, forgiveness, guidance, and strength. I desire to make God's will my own and to be obedient to it. I desire to remain in Christ with the help of this covenant so that I might bear fruit for the kingdom of God.

Our group acknowledges the call of Jesus Christ to be his disciples. We dedicate ourselves to a life that exemplifies faithful and loving obedience to God through balance of mind, body, and spirit; support of one another; and our witness in the world. With God's grace we will . . .

To be a Christian disciple means sharing in Christ's ongoing work of salvation in the world. The task of discipleship therefore calls for the binding together of those with like mind and purpose to watch over one another in love. We covenant together to be present each week. We will open and close our meetings with prayer to help focus our minds and hearts on God rather than on ourselves and our accomplishments. We will approach one another with honesty and in a spirit of love. Understanding that our purpose is not to judge one another, we will strive to speak honestly in terms of both our keeping with the covenant and our failure to do so. As Christ does for us, so will we try to the best of our ability to watch over one another in love. We covenant together to offer encouragement to one another to grow in faith.

Acknowledging the tension of experiencing divine absence and presence, we nevertheless affirm that our God is faithful, redemptive, and gracious. We seek to respond faithfully through acts of compassion, justice, devotion, and worship. Empowered by the Holy Spirit and in community with the whole church, we strive to be disciples of our Lord Jesus Christ. We therefore commit ourselves to the following disciplines: . . .

Having been called by the mystery of God, using the gifts we have been given and empowered by our sense of responsibility that recognizes the inherent worth and dignity of every individual, we pledge ourselves to living as disciples; receiving grace for ourselves and others through acts of compassion, justice, worship, and devotion; and developing a lifelong practice of carrying out these acts of grace so that we may all grow in love and harmony. With God's grace and each other's help, we covenant to . . .

We celebrate God's bringing us together by grace and mercy through the life, death, and resurrection of Jesus Christ, by whom we are called to be disciples. Our lives have been changed as we have turned to God through Jesus Christ, the source of our faith and the indwelling of the Holy Spirit. We covenant together to exemplify Christ's vision for the church, reaching out to everyone as a sign and servant of Christ.

In search of a place where we can share our spiritual journey with one another, we come together in covenant to encourage one another in faith. We acknowledge that the road we travel as disciples of Christ is sometimes difficult during both discovery and navigation. Therefore, we will meet weekly to offer one another our love, prayers, and support. With God's grace and our mutual accountability we will . . .

In the great mystery of God's love, we are called into being, redeemed, and empowered for God's suffering and service in transforming the world. We humbly offer our time, abilities, resources, brokenness, and will to God in order that God's kingdom may bear fruit in us and in the world. Seeking God's kingdom, we commit our time and presence to this Covenant Discipleship Group to watch over one another in love. We will witness to Jesus Christ in the world and follow Jesus' teachings.

Examples of Covenant Clauses

Acts of Compassion

- I will do all I can to help people in need.
- I will seek out people in need and do all I can to help them.
- We will strive to increase our service to others and graciously acknowledge others' service to us.
- I will go two miles for a sister or a brother who asks me to go one.
- I will spend one hour each week visiting a "hugless" person whom I would not ordinarily visit.
- I will spend at least one hour each day helping someone in need.
- I will spend four hours each month helping disadvantaged people in my community.
- I will spend four hours each week helping disadvantaged people in my community.
- We will balance the time we devote to school, church, work, family, and friends, including our own spiritual and recreational life.
- I will spend an hour each day with my children.
- I will spend some time each day in meaningful communication with each member of my family.
- We will practice listening to other people as a ministry of grace.
- I will express genuine appreciation to at least one person each day.
- We will engage in regular visits to local prisons.
- I will make weekly visits to local prisons.
- We will each establish a meaningful relationship with someone in prison, and, where possible, with their families.
- I will get to know at least one family that lives at the poverty level of income.
- I will offer friendship each day to someone of an ethnic background different from my own.

- We will encourage our congregation in its missional giving by our own personal example.
- I will seek to help a family in need somewhere else in the world.
- I will eat one less meal each day and give the money to feed the hungry.
- I will improve meaningful communications with my family.
- We will be alert for opportunities to reflect Christ to those with whom we come into contact.
- At least twice weekly I will seek to offer compassionate service and encouragement to those outside my normal circle of contacts.
- At least twice weekly I will seek to offer compassionate service and encouragement to those inside my normal circle of contacts.
- I will affirm the God-given gifts of others.

Acts of Justice

- I will endeavor to oppose injustice, in whatever form.
- When I am aware of injustices practiced in my church, my community, my nation, and the world, I will speak out.
- We will not be silent when confronted with social injustice; and we will witness for justice, inclusiveness, and equality and will encourage reconciliation wherever possible.
- I will stand up for those who are not present or able to stand up for themselves.
- I will actively support a movement for world peace.
- I will communicate regularly with my elected national representatives on issues of world peace.
- I will get to know at least one unemployed person.
- I will communicate regularly with my elected local representatives on issues of unemployment and economic justice.

- I will get to know at least one person of a different ethnic background at my place of work.
- We will become more aware of social situations through attention to the news (newspapers, television, magazines, radio).
- I will ask forgiveness of God each day for those who die of starvation, and I will work to alleviate world hunger.
- We will become an advocacy group for prisoners of religious and political conscience.
- As a group, we will speak out whenever God's justice is ignored by our leaders at work, at church, in our nation, and in the world.
- In the coming year our daily Bible study will include the prophets Amos, Hosea, Micah, and Isaiah.
- I will dissociate myself from racial slurs and jokes at my place of work.
- I will express disapproval of racial, social, and sexual prejudice among my relatives and friends.
- We will practice responsible stewardship of the world's resources in the context of our personal lives and communal commitments.
- I will strive for unconditional love and acceptance of all God's creations.
- We will acknowledge all people as God's creation regardless of socioeconomic or ethnic background.
- We will accept God's charge to exercise dominion over all the earth and will share this task of being God's stewards by practicing conservation of the earth's natural resources for the well-being of both current and future generations.
- We will take action at least once a month that directly affects individuals in a way that may have impact on a wider issue of justice or a root cause of injustice.
- I will pray every day for the coming of the reign of God.

Acts of Devotion

- We will practice daily devotions, including reading Scripture and praying for group members.
- I will pray each day, privately and publicly.
- I will spend at least one hour each day in the disciplines of praise, thanksgiving, confession, petition, intercession, and meditation.
- I will pray daily in solitude and with my family or friends. I will include all the members of my Covenant Discipleship Group in my daily prayers.
- I will keep a diary to plan my daily and weekly prayers.
- We will make the study of Scripture a central part of our daily devotions.
- We will read common daily Bible readings and share our insights as we give an account each week.
- I will record the spiritual insights of my daily Bible reading.
- I will read the Bible each day as a devotional exercise and not a study assignment.
- We will learn the discipline of journaling.
- We will each keep a spiritual journal and will devote time at the end of each day to enter our reflections as the Holy Spirit leads us.
- I will spend at least thirty minutes each day alone with God, of which fifteen minutes will be spent just listening to God.
- I will pray each day for my enemies.
- I will take the initiative each day in holding family devotions.
- I will read only those materials and watch only those programs that enhance my discipleship.
- I prayerfully pledge to practice responsible stewardship of my God-given resources: my body, artistic graces, and intellectual gifts.
- In order to care for our wholeness in body, mind, and spirit, we will schedule time each week for retreat, reflection, renewal, and fun.

- Knowing that my body is the temple of God, I will prayerfully plan my work and leisure time.
- I will seek the guidance of the Holy Spirit in fasting.
- I will use traveling time for prayer and reflection.
- We will include our children in acts of devotion.
- I will memorize a verse of Scripture each day.
- We will contribute one tenth of all our income to church or charity.
- We will daily and thankfully practice the presence of God with us through prayer and meditation, seeking to grow in the knowledge and love of God.
- I will pray daily for a person in need and will keep a list of those whom I know to be in need.
- We will offer prayers of adoration and thanksgiving without asking anything of God.

Acts of Worship

- I will be faithful in attendance and participation in worship each Sunday.
- We will participate in weekly corporate worship, striving for true involvement.
- I will seek opportunities for worship at least once each week in addition to Sunday.
- I will receive the sacrament of Holy Communion each week.
- We will receive the sacrament of Holy Communion daily.
- We will prayerfully consider what resources we can contribute each week to the work of Christ in the world.
- I will return to Christ the first tenth of all that I receive.
- We will pray for those who lead us in worship each week, and especially for the preacher.
- We will pray for those who visit our worship service, that they will be touched by grace.

- We will pray for those who are baptized in our church, and we will visit the parents of baptized children.
- We will seek to experience forms of worship different from our own tradition.
- I will seek to cross racial boundaries in worship.

Spiritual Promptings and Warnings

- I will listen to the promptings of the Spirit as they affect others' well-being.
- I will witness to my faith in Christ at least once each day.
- I will remember that whatever I do—be it work, study, or recreation—is dedicated to God.
- I will be truthful to my Covenant Discipleship Group whenever I disobey a spiritual prompting or fail to heed a spiritual warning.
- I will set aside a specific time for personal spiritual renewal each week.
- As a group we will spend a day in retreat twice each year.
- We will be available to one another at all times for support and prayer in times of spiritual testing.
- I will not let the sun set on my anger.
- We will listen to that still small voice from God and seek to learn from God's mysterious presence in all of life.
- I will try to live each day in the knowledge that God's spirit is within me and available to me.
- Since our tongue is like the rudder of a ship, we will try to recognize the warnings of the Holy Spirit when our words should remain unspoken.

Examples of Covenant Conclusions

Knowing that the grace of God works in each of us, I pray that my heart be opened to God's presence, that my eyes be opened to see the sorrows and joys of God's creatures, and that my ears be opened to hear God's will so that I will have the strength to keep this covenant.

By affixing my signature to this document, the singular "I" becomes the communal "We." We therefore pledge our commitment to God and to the group, that the choices we make in our daily journeys will enhance our growth as Christians, honor our Creator and Redeemer, and minister to our world.

Recognizing that there are times when we cannot live up to the standards we have set for ourselves, we covenant to support one another in an encouraging and constructive manner.

Trusting in grace, we pledge to support one another as we leave the confines of comfort in our search to do God's will in the world.

Covenant Worksheet

Preamble

Clauses

Acts of Compassion

Acts of Justice

Acts of Devotion

Acts of Worship

Spiritual Promptings and Warnings

Conclusion

Preamble

In gratitude for the grace of Jesus Christ, in whose death we have died and in whose resurrection we have found new life, we pledge to be his disciples. We recognize that our time and talents are gifts from God, and we will use them to search out God's will for us and to obey. We will do our best not to compromise the will of God for human goals. We will serve both God and God's creation earnestly and lovingly. We respect and accept fully all group members, whose integrity and confidentiality we will uphold in all that we share. With God's grace and their help, we make our covenant.

Clauses

Acts of Compassion

I will spend four hours each month helping the poor people in my community.

Acts of Justice

When I am aware of injustice to others, I will not remain silent.

Acts of Devotion

I will pray each day, privately and with family or friends.
I will read and study the Scriptures each day.
I will prayerfully care for my body and for the world in which I live.
I will return to Christ the first tenth of all I receive.

Acts of Worship

I will worship each Sunday, unless prevented.
I will receive the sacrament of Holy Communion each week.

Spiritual Promptings and Warnings

I will obey the promptings of the Holy Spirit to serve God and my neighbor.
I will heed the warnings of the Holy Spirit not to sin against God and my neighbor.

Conclusion

I hereby make my commitment, trusting in the grace of God to give me the will and the strength to keep this covenant.

Signed: _____

Date: _____

Practicing the Basics of Discipleship

Following is a list of some of the acts of discipleship in which students at Wesley Theological Seminary took part while they were in Covenant Discipleship Groups during a typical academic year.

Acts of Compassion

Delivered food and toys to needy families
Visited hospitals to sing for patients
Listened to the bereaved
Helped with a feeding program
Worked at a homeless shelter
Taught in a program for homeless people
Visited homebound people in my church
Visited those who stopped by the church
Ushered at the funeral of a classmate's father
Helped with a hospital pet therapy program
Corresponded with a prison inmate
Visited at a hospice
Reached out to those who irritate me
Assisted a newcomer to the USA in settling
Participated in ministry to women in prison
Shared personal possessions with those in need
Regularly helped a person with disabilities
Made friends with a person who has AIDS

Acts of Justice

Supported the Board of Child Care
Helped to translate in court for those who
   could not speak English
Organized immigration workshop
Contributed to outreach programs
Organized a project to collect school supplies
Registered as a Child Advocate
Brought justice issues into sermons
Fed hungry people
Became more alert to inclusive language
Became aware of a crisis-pregnancy center
Worked with senior citizens
Wrote letters to Congress on justice issues
Attended conference on children's needs
Spoke out against prejudice and rudeness
Read newspapers more intentionally
Pledged financial support for a missionary
Refrained from gossiping
Attended a meeting on church revitalization

Acts of Devotion

Scheduled a quiet time each morning
Used songs and music in personal devotion
Sang spirituals as prayer
Included my children in acts of devotion
Kept a spiritual journal
Memorized some Scripture
Found moments of joy throughout the day
Wrote poetry and prose that praised God
Balanced time with fun, work, and family
Led devotionals with church youth
Joined a spiritual support group
Burned a devotional candle
Used modeling clay in prayer
Tried for true involvement in church
Began each day with a song of praise
Read Scripture before going to morning class
Prayed for those in conflict with me
Observed regular days of fasting

Acts of Worship

Experienced new forms of worship
Attended worship on campus regularly
Prayed for leaders of worship services
Took Communion every time it was offered
Prayed for visitors and newcomers at worship
Began taking notes in worship
Worshiped with an inclusive congregation
Began to tithe
Remembered God in nature walks
Visited other churches twice a month
Led and participated in a foot-washing service
Participated regularly as a worship leader
Took part in choir on campus
Worshiped with imprisoned women
Worked with youth to do Easter sunrise service
Became more involved when leading services
Started a monthly Bible study in my house
Included prayers for the broader community

To witness to Jesus Christ in the world, and to follow his teachings through acts of compassion, justice, worship, and devotion, under the guidance of the Holy Spirit.

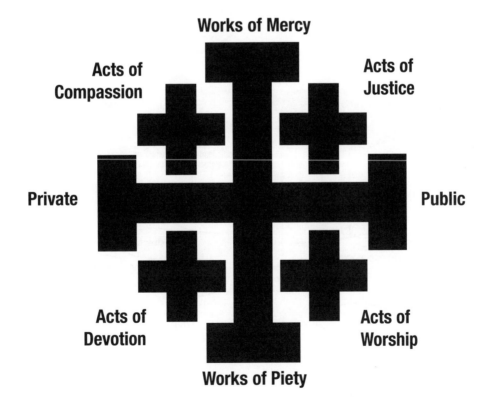

Accountable Discipleship Canopy

Covenant Discipleship Groups are part of a larger ministry of accountable discipleship. The diagram below indicates a sampling of the many groups and settings that fall within the canopy of accountable discipleship. If you are interested in finding out more about any of the groups listed below, contact the Office of Accountable Discipleship, General Board of Discipleship, P.O. Box 340003, Nashville, TN 37203-0003, phone 1-877-899-2780, extension 1765.

Covenant Discipleship Quarterly is a quarterly newsletter for members of Covenant Discipleship Groups. It can be found on the General Board of Discipleship Web site (www.gbod.org), or you can receive a free subscription by writing to Covenant Discipleship Quarterly, P.O. Box 340003, Nashville, TN 37203-0003; by calling toll-free 1-877-899-2780, extension 7144; or by e-mailing jeslinger@gbod.org.

The following resources can by ordered from Discipleship Resources at 1-800-685-4370 or www.discipleshipresources.org, or from Cokesbury at 1-800-672-1789.

Accountable Discipleship: Living in God's Household, by Steve Manskar (Discipleship Resources, 2000).

Guide for Class Leaders: A Model for Christian Formation, by Grace Bradford (Discipleship Resources, 1999).

Sprouts: Nurturing Children Through Covenant Discipleship, by Edie Genung Harris and Shirley L. Ramsey (Discipleship Resources, 1995).

Together in Love: Covenant Discipleship With Youth, by David Sutherland (Discipleship Resources, 1999).

The following resources can be ordered from Upper Room Books at 1-800-972-0433 or http://bookstore.upperroom.org, or from Cokesbury at 1-800-672-1789.

A Guide to Prayer for Ministers and Other Servants, by Rueben P. Job and Norman Shawchuck (Upper Room Books, 1983).

A Guide to Spiritual Discernment, by Rueben P. Job (Upper Room Books, 1996).

Hunger of the Heart: A Workbook, by Ron DelBene with Mary and Herb Montgomery (Upper Room Books, 1995).

Devotional Life in the Wesleyan Tradition, by Steve Harper (Upper Room Books, 1983). Also available in workbook format.

Learning to Listen: A Guide for Spiritual Friends, by Wendy Miller (Upper Room Books, 1993).

The following resources can be ordered from Cokesbury at 1-800-672-1789.

A Wesleyan Spiritual Reader, by Rueben P. Job (Abingdon Press, 1997).

Celebration of Discipline: The Path to Spiritual Growth, by Richard J. Foster (Harper & Row, 1988). Study guide available.

For questions or additional information on Covenant Discipleship Groups, see the General Board of Discipleship Web site (www.gbod.org) or contact the Office of Accountable Discipleship, General Board of Discipleship, P.O. Box 340003, Nashville, TN 37203-0003, phone 1-877-899-2780, extension 1765.

Notes